From Decline to Deliverance

Helping Pastors to Grow Declining Churches

by

Dr. Thomas Dawson Jr.

In memory of Reverend Jonathan L. Murray, who served as my Assistant Pastor for 23 years. My dear friend was truly a humble and loyal servant for the Lord. He was a quiet yet powerful influencer. He traveled around the country with me without hesitation, which resulted in the SOAR Church becoming the contemporary ministry it is today. I thank God for him and the impact he has had on my life and our SOAR Church family.

Acknowledgements

First, I want to thank God for His privilege of being used in His Kingdom for such a time as this. These are exciting times to do ministry and I want to thank God for His unusual favor upon my life. I have a desire to help pastors and churches to grow in this season and I am grateful for the opportunity to write this book.

To my wife Adriane and daughter Alexandria, thank you for the sacrifice you have made during my time in ministry over the past twenty-two years. Thank you for your strength and support; they have meant the world to me. To my Dawson family and friends, much love to you and thank you for your support.

To my SOAR Nation family, you have meant the world to me. Thank you for allowing me to serve you as pastor. You have always encouraged and supported the big vision that God has given me. You have pushed me to be the best that I could be, and I pray that I have made you proud. Your unwavering support has allowed me to go through doors that I never dreamed I could walk through. To Deaconess Nina Hendricks and Crystal Brown, I thank you for helping me with this project. Without you this would not be possible.

Finally, I would like to dedicate this book to my brother Damon Dawson, niece Damonic Dawson, and my mother-in-law Marilyn Redfern, who always encouraged me in ministry and as her pastor. You three inspired me to go and impact this world for Jesus Christ.

Table of Contents

Chapter 1

Introduction

The occupation of Senior Pastor has become challenging over the past few years, challenging because many churches across America appear to be struggling with church attendance. This has contributed to a decline in many churches, thereby, causing many to close their doors.

Dr. Richard J. Kreger presents some statistics and reasons he believes have caused churches to decline in America. Dr. Kreger states, "Every year more than 4,000 churches closed their doors compared to just over 1,000 new church starts.[1]" He reports that every year 2.7 million church members fall into inactivity. It appears that people are leaving churches in larger numbers or just not participating as they have in the past. It is important for the churches to know what is causing the decline in membership as that decline hinders the Kingdom of God from growing.

The church where I serve as pastor, The SOAR Church of Woodbine, had experienced decline prior to his arrival in 1998. The church, formerly called First Baptist Church of Woodbine, was considered a declining church because

---

[1] Dr. Richard J. Krejcir, What is Going on with Pastor in America? Schaeffer Institute of Church Leadership development

there was no growth numerically. In addition, there was an absence of ministry and community outreach within the church. Their style of ministry was considered traditional as was the case with other churches in this rural area of Southern New Jersey. The term "traditional ministry" can be defined as a ministry approach that consists of hymns, choirs, organs, long worship services, long sermons, mission programs, and annual-day services throughout the year, all designed to raise financial support for the church. It was a Christian tradition that had been passed down generationally. They were stuck in the past with no vision for the future.

There was very little outreach to the community which meant that the Great Commission in Matthew 28:18-20, "Go, ye, therefore, and teach all nations, baptizing them in the name of Father, and the Son, and of the Holy Spirit" was not being fulfilled. The Great Commission was not a focus during that time. The church was program driven, not worship driven. Church membership, numbering approximately sixty people weekly for Sunday worship services and fewer than twenty for mid-week services, had not experienced any sustainable growth prior to my arrival. It was a church that had a pastor resign after two years because of conflict. In addition, there were not many families nor youth present during that time despite the church's 90-year existence and long-standing history in that community.

This church, in a town of approximately 2,000 residents, is in a rural southern New Jersey multi-cultural town. Formerly, the church had a congregation that consisted of only African- American membership; however, when I came onboard as the new senior pastor, I began to implement the vision that God had given me for this ministry. At this time – the early 2000's - the church started to experience growth and expansion. The Bible is clear in Proverbs 29:18: "Where there is no vision, the people perish." A pastoral vision is necessary because it allows the church to know what they stand for, who they are, and where they are going. A vision gives the church direction and serves as a road map. Habakkuk 2:2: "Write the vision and make it plain upon the tables that he may run that readeth it." The pastor and leadership made the vision plain and the congregation ran with it.

As pastor, I was given a vision by God to transform the direction of the ministry and to a focus more in the direction of the Great Commission mentioned in Matthew 28:18-20. During this transition, the church changed its ministry philosophy to focus on evangelism and community outreach. The evangelism consisted of reaching individuals with the gospel message by meeting needs with food distribution, clothing giveaways, school supplies distributions, and autism awareness and support to local schools. The church has also partnered with local schools and local law enforcement, all of which helped its outreach efforts. The pastor, leadership, and congregation, after much prayer concerning the pastor's vision and the leading by the Holy Spirt, decided to change its direction which started a growth process.

The church changed its name from First Baptist Church of Woodbine to The SOAR Church in the year 2010. The name SOAR, an acronym for Soldiers Order after Righteousness, reflects the vision that was implemented and communicates that we are believers who are following the righteousness of God and growing into having a right relationship with God. The Bible says in 2 Peter 3:18, "But grow in the grace and knowledge of our Lord and Savior Jesus Christ." The Bible also says in Romans 12:2, "...and be not conformed to this world but be ye transformed by the renewing of your mind that you may prove what is that acceptable and perfect will of God." These are the verses that are used to support the SOAR Church's vision.

The pastor and leadership believe that the name should reflect what the ministry is about and where it is heading. The SOAR Church's vision is about reaching, reproducing, reclaiming, and rebuilding families for Jesus Christ. In so doing, the church has become one of the fastest growing churches in the area with 300 in weekly attendance. It has changed from African- American membership only to multi-cultural membership reflecting the community it serves. As the senior pastor I believe that the church should indeed reflect the community it serves, and because of that, the SOAR Church has become a place of worship for multi-cultural families from its community. The new direction has enabled the church to become more family-oriented meeting the needs of the entire family. Because of this transition in purpose, I believe that this study can help many churches experiencing a decline begin to experience growth both spiritually and numerically.

There Is a Problem

As a senior pastor, I have seen many churches in the Southern New Jersey and the Philadelphia areas that are either declining or have closed over the past several years. This problem is impacting churches in both urban and rural areas and in all denominations such as Baptist, Pentecostal, and Non-denominational churches. It is a problem that is seen with all cultures and in all communities. This is a problem being experienced across the United States of America, a problem that has many pastors confused when it comes to the issue of declining churches.

I recently talked to a pastor in the same New Jersey county as the church where he serves. This pastor had recently been installed as senior pastor to a church already in decline with a membership of thirty, and after his arrival, the membership decreased to 12 in weekly attendance after his presence on the job for ten months. The pastor believed that this church would close soon because the membership could not afford to manage its facilities; he did not have an answer to its decline. The church is in a well-populated area but there did not seem to be a viable means to grow the church. This pastor began searching for a new church in a different area.

Tony Morgan wrote a book that is designed to equip churches to experience sustained health and growth. He writes in his book entitled *The Unstuck Church* that churches have a life cycle like people. He says, "Eventually it reaches a plateau, and if nothing is done to move it, it begins to decline. If nothing interrupts the decline, it will die.[2]" The church must have plan in place to move it forward so that it will not experience a decline. Many pastors and leadership do not have a plan in place to turn around their church decline. Tony Morgan, who works with church leaders across the United States of America every day, says, "Here's what I know to be true, churches all around you are stuck.3" This is a problem that is seen in every city and community. If it is seen in every city and community, then the consequence is that these areas will suffer from lack of community outreach and the paucity of the gospel being presented to the lost.

There is a pastor, a close friend, who serves as senior pastor to a church in another county in Southern New Jersey. He has expressed his concerns regarding the decline that his church has experienced. When he arrived at this church twelve years ago, the church had a membership of seventy-five in weekly attendance. Today, this church has a weekly attendance of twenty. This pastor is very well trained in the Bible and preaches dynamically; however, he has no answer for the decline. He even talked of possibly retiring from the pastoral ministry soon.

Thom S. Rainer addresses the decline of churches in his book entitled *Autopsy of the Church*. He concludes that in some churches decline is everywhere but somehow people do not see it. His point is that the decline is due to the past; churches are stuck in the past. Thom S. Rainer says,

---

[2] Tony Morgan, The Unstuck Church, Thomas Nelson Publishers

"They were fighting for the past, the good old days and the way it used to be.[3]" Many churches are declining today because the past is their hero; the past means more to them than the future. This decline is seen in the condition of the physical building, the spiritual growth of the members, and outreach to the community.

In addition, I have interviewed pastors of small-to-medium-sized churches, I recently talked to a pastor of a mega church in the New Jersey area recently. This church had a weekly attendance of 4,000 and was one of the fastest growing churches in New Jersey during the late 1990's and early 2000's. Today, this church has experienced a substantial decline where the church is seeing a weekly attendance of 2000. The problem of decline is experienced in small churches as well as mega churches. This is a problem that does not discriminate which it comes to the size or culture of a ministry.

I have seen the same problem in Philadelphia, Pennsylvania, one urban area where churches big and small are dealing with the same issue of decline. I have recently seen a close pastor friend who died of a heart attack as he was attempting to grow his church and deal with the pressures and problems of ministry. His congregation was small, and he was trying to grow it and keep it from declining. In another instance, I had another close pastor friend who committed suicide after dealing with personal problems and suffering through the loss of

[3] Thom S. Rainer, Autopsy of the Church, B&H Publishing Group

support from many in membership. He wanted to grow the church but his problems and people leaving the ministry caused pain and hurt in his life. The pressure to produce and grow a church can cause many problems in the life of a pastor.

Thom S. Rainer confirms that similar actions seen in Haggai Chapter 1 are evident in declining churches today. He performs an autopsy on fourteen declining churches, all of which displayed the actions that were present in Haggai Chapter 1. First, Rainer observes that they moved their focus from others to themselves. He says, "When a church moves in that direction, it is headed for decline, then death.[4]" When there is a decline, the church will stop growing and people are not coming to God. There is also a lack of spiritual growth and communities are no longer reached with the Gospel of Jesus Christ. These actions are just some of the contributors to church decline. Most of these churches operating in these manners are unaware that they can lead to a decline. God addressed it in Haggai and wants this issue addressed today. Modern-day churches must be aware of both these problems and the solutions needed to correct the problem of decline.

Daniel Burke, the religion writer for CNN, wrote an article titled "10 Reasons Americans Go to Church and 9 Reasons They Don't.[5]" He states, "If American religion

---

[4] Thom S. Rainer, Autopsy of the Church, B&H Publishing Group

[5] [5] Daniel Burke, 10 Reasons Americans Go to Church, CNN

were traded at the stock exchange, your broker might be advising you to sell." He believes that trends do not look great and have not for some time. He quoted 4,729 Americans surveyed by the new Pew Research Center stating the following reasons for not attending church services: They practice their faith (37%); they are not believers (28%); they have not found a house of worship they like (23%); they do not like the sermons (18%); they do not feel welcome (14%), and no house of worship in their area (7%). The church, if it is going to turn around, must understand what it takes to reach a lost generation.

This book is important because many pastors are struggling regarding how to move their churches forward. If pastors are struggling with their role as senior pastors, how can churches grow spiritually and numerically? It has been noticed in the Southern New Jersey area that churches that have strong leadership with Pastors and Deacons and who are united in following their God-given vision are experiencing growth. Ed Stetzer in an article for *Christianity Today* says, "Pastors Are all Miserable and Want to Quit.[6]" He presents some statistics that try to prove that many pastors want to quit because of the stress and pressure of ministry using research done by Barna Research and Focus on the Family. Statistics concerning the stress of the pastoral ministry state that 80% of pastors feel unqualified and discouraged; 72% of pastors report working between 55 to 75 hours per week, and 50% of

---

[6] Ed Stetzer, Pastors are miserable and want to quit, Christianity Today.

pastors are so discouraged that they would leave the ministry. The problem of growing a church can be stressful on all involved. This could be one of the indicators as to why churches may be experiencing a decline. Everything rises and falls with leadership. It appears that a decline can impact many areas of the church, its leadership, its membership, and the communities these churches serve.

Is the Church Really Dead?

This book was written because despite many churches being on the decline, one small church in a rural town of New Jersey reversed its decline by changing its ministry philosophy. The change implemented by the pastor and leadership impacted not only this small church but also the entire county where it is located. The SOAR Church experienced growth while other churches in the same county underwent decline. The purpose of this book is to help pastors and churches see they too can reverse the problem of decline or being stuck. It has been demonstrated by The SOAR Church and many other churches across this country that this problem can be fixed.

There has been a great deal of discussion lately concerning church attendance. Many churches are experiencing a huge drop in visitors. Jayson D. Bradley wrote an article that presented statistics from the last twenty years concerning a drop-in church attendance. In his article entitled *6 Important Church Attendance Statistics and What They Truly Tell Us*," Bradley believes that church attendance has been decline for some time. He says, "In 1992, 70 percent of Americans claim to be regular attendees in a house of worship. Less than 35 years later, that number had dropped to 55 percent who claim they regularly attend a house of worship.[7]" Based on these statistics, the church has been experiencing a decline for some time and is not a problem that has presented itself in the past few years. This ongoing problem was not addressed and appears to be getting worse. If the church is going to grow as God intended, then the problem of church decline must be addressed.

As pastor, I have observed several churches within the same Southern New Jersey area. These statistics are evident in this county as churches continue to decline with no answers to reverse it. I observed that several churches in that county over the past five years have experienced little to no growth, with two of these churches having closed recently. Moreover, I observed that many of these pastors have had difficulty in coming up with a plan to reverse this problem. These churches are representative of all denominations.

On the other hand, there was an observation that four churches are growing and thriving within the same county, and these churches are located within miles of the ones that are stuck and experiencing a decline. All these

---

[7] Jayson D, Bradley, 6 Important Church Attendance Statistics and What they Truly Tell Us

churches are Biblically based and serving the same God but are coming up with different results. The purpose of this book is to help churches that may be miles apart physically and spiritually to experience the same results of growth when it comes to ministry. This book seeks to show that with the right vision and plan any church can experience growth numerically and physically. As a pastor and leader, I have been told by many believers and leaders that only "church plants" are the churches that are growing in today's society. As a pastor and leader, I have seen many pastors leave existing churches to plant their own church. Some of these pastors have experienced tremendous growth.

Dr. R. A Vernon, who serves as Senior Pastor of the Word Church in Cleveland, Ohio, started that church after being asked to leave a church that rejected his leadership and vision. He started The Word Church twenty years ago and has several thousand members and three locations. In his book entitled *The Blessing Behind Closed Doors,* Vernon says, "You can imagine how frustrating it was for me to have to come to the entire congregation to vote on vision.[8]" He explains how he felt dispirited after that process. Once being free from that process, he was able to do what God called him to do and experience tremendous growth. Many pastors, tired of fighting with leadership for vision and direction, would rather plant. They are of the

---

[8] Dr. R. A. Vernon, The Blessings Behind Closed Doors, Victory media and Publishing

mindset that planting is the way to grow their ministries. Dr. R. A Vernon trains hundreds of pastors every year in church growth strategies.

In addition, I have observed a church plant in Trenton, New Jersey, which has several thousand members. Ten years ago, this same pastor had been rejected because of his leadership at his former church; he was asked to leave. Despite that, he was able to implement a vision with his leadership at his Trenton church plant and it resulted in a growing church. A leadership that is divided can hinder churches from experiencing growth, while these examples of church plants are experiencing tremendous growth. It has been noticed that churches where there is unity between the pastor and leadership are experiencing growth. These types of churches have also used creative ways in reaching people for the Kingdom of God. They use social media, technology, drama, shorter services, and creative sermons.

I do not believe that only church plants will experience growth, though. I have observed church plants in Southern New Jersey and the Philadelphia, Pennsylvania, area that experience a decline. These church plants have been in existence for decades or more yet have had difficulty growing their ministries. In contrast, from my observation I have seen existing churches turn around and experience growth. This book is designed to help existing churches and church plants reverse declines so they can experience growth.

Another purpose of this book is to help pastors to grow churches. As a pastor, I want to help other pastors with a plan and a strategy to fix this problem of decline. Pastors must see that there is a solution to their churches' stagnation. Dr. R A Vernon in his book *Size Does Matter* communicates that it is up to the pastor and leadership to follow a God-given vision for that particular area on how it is going to reach the people. Dr. R A Vernon further states, "People come to be fed spiritually and if the food isn't good, chances are they will look to another church.[9]" People go where they can grow spiritually and where their needs can be met. A church with a vision for reaching people will grow and make disciples for the Kingdom of God.

Jeremiah 3:15 reads, "I will give you shepherds after my own heart which shall feed you with knowledge and skill." It is God who places pastors in the local church to teach the people and to grow the church spiritually. Churches are declining because many pastors are not fulfilling what God said in Jeremiah 3:15. They have been called to the local church to feed the flock, but they have not been equipped to carry out that function. Dr. Tony Evans believes that pastors are attempting to lead outside spiritual guidelines. Numerous pastors have gotten away from the Bible when it comes to leading the church. He states in his book entitled *Let's Get to Know Each Other*

---

[9] Dr. R.A. Vernon Size Does matter: Moving Your Ministry from Micro to Mega. Victory Media & Publishing Company

that the "Spiritual has taken a secondary role to the social and political in recent years.[10]"

Because of a lack of Biblical development, many pastors have not helped the local church to grow spiritually. Ephesians 6:11 – 16 outlines how the church is to equip the congregation for the work of the ministry. Carlyle Feilding Stewart believes that as pastors become more educated, the problems of their role of being ill-equipped to pastor are dispelled. He states that "people seek a church that not only inspires and uplifts but one that challenges the mind through sound educational programs and good Christian teaching.[11]" People today want to be challenged in the Word of God. When pastors are not equipped, the church suffers and start to decline.

The position of senior pastor is a position that carries a great deal of responsibility. The pastor has been placed in that position by God, a calling and not something an individual decides to do. The pastor is to help the church to carry out its commission found in Matthew 28:18-20, "Go teach and make disciples." Churches have deviated from that commission and the role of the church. Carlyle Feilding Stewart told of a story of a young man who left his local church because the pastor displayed a negative role, one contrary to that charged in the Bible. He said, "The pastor spent too much time beating up his

---

[10] Dr. Tony Evans, Let's Get to Know Each Other, Thomas Nelson Publishers

[11] Carlyle Feilding Stewart, African American church growth, Abingdon Press

congregation from the pulpit.[12]" The behavior demonstrated by this pastor and others like him will contribute to the decline of a church. The pulpit is designed to build up individuals and not to tear them down.

What Is Church Decline?

This book is intended to be both scriptural and practical in application. This book is from a research that seeks to give people a better understanding of the problem of declining churches, the reasons for the decline, the lack of understanding on how to grow churches, and the skills needed to reverse the decline in church attendance/member numbers and actual folding of churches. Can this book help other pastors with declining numbers experience growth? Can this research help pastors with a plan and strategy for growth? Is there hope for the many churches that are declining in the United States of America? The purpose of the book is to answers those questions.

This book will develop assumptions based on viewpoints, necessary biases, and theoretical precedents. These assumptions will aid in the understanding and presentation of this research and bring to light how this subject is viewed in public. As we acknowledge the viewpoints of this research, several positive views have been developed. Based on my experience as a senior pastor in several styles of ministries, I have found that churches can fix the

---

[12] Carlyle Feilding Stewart, African American church growth, Abingdon Press

problem of decline and experience turn around and growth.

I am excited to research the issue of declining churches because churches need help in transitioning today. I have experience with both contemporary and traditional types of churches, and my hope is that this book will help some churches to grow and likewise become effective in their community whether rural or urban.

What Is Needed to Help Declining Churches?

This book is being executed and directed toward mainline churches but is more applicable in the Baptist Church, Church of God in Christ, and non-denominational circles. Designed to address the issues of church decline, this study will bring understanding and tools to churches in decline in denominational circles and cultures. This book on declining churches is an extensive study that can have a variety of responses and conclusions depending on the vision and ministry styles of individual churches. In this book, I will refer to a traditional style in many instances because the writer has a background in traditional ministry which many churches continue to use.

This book, however, will not compare churches to see which is right or wrong, but it will look at certain styles to see what is effective during this time. It will attempt to offer ideas about combating the decline in the nation's churches and reversing that trend to begin growing churches; that way, understanding, worship, service, and meeting needs as the commission compels will be satisfied. God is a God of diversity and the Gospel of

Jesus Christ is a gospel of grace, not of race nor of comparison and competition. When God created the church, He had everyone in mind with no one theological practice better than another if the unadulterated word of God is preached and taught. Again, this book will often refer to a traditional style of ministry in this research because it has played a major role in the local church.

This book, however, will not criticize any generations or culture. The Apostle Paul says in I Corinthians 9:22, "To the weak I became as weak, that I might gain the weak: I am made all things to all men, that I might by all means save some." Paul transitioned his ministry style often so that he could relate to the different cultures he encountered in order to win them for Christ. The church is called to relate to the different cultures and generations that it may encounter along this journey. Just as a traditional ministry style may relate to one generation, a contemporary style may relate to another generation or culture. The many ministry styles within Christianity should have one goal in mind and that is to gain more for the Kingdom of God.

There are over 2,000 active faiths in the United States, but this book will not criticize any of these faiths. The premise is twofold, that people need different types of faiths and that people worship God in their way. The purpose of worship whether it is contemporary, traditional, or another style of faith is to help people to be in a right relationship with God. Matthew 6:33 addresses this issue with, "But seek ye first the kingdom of God, and His righteousness and all these things shall be added unto you." It is about putting God first; different faiths should not be at war over which style is right or wrong. If a faith is helping people in their relationship with God, then it should not be criticized.

The purpose of the church through its various denominations and faiths is to reach people right where they are. Denominations serve that purpose because it takes a variety to reach so many cultures in our communities and country. The church must have a sense of call to the community. No matter what denomination the ministries of the local church operate under, ministry should be designed to relate to the culture within that community. The church where I serve as pastor has designed ministries that fit needs - feed the hungry, provide clothing, and serve broken families because the community consists of people with these issues. All churches should carry out the Biblical mandate in Matthew 25:35, "For I hungered and ye gave me meat: I was thirsty and ye gave me drink: I was a stranger, and ye took me in."

While this book will not disparage faiths, styles of worship, or ministry approaches, neither will it condemn any senior pastor. The position of a pastor is very powerful and carries great responsibility. It represents the authority of God, and it is the Lord God, who picks a pastor and places him in a local church. His role is to mature, mend, and instruct believers in the Word of God. The pastor's purpose is to carry out the great commission found in Matthew 28:18-20, "Go ye therefore and teach all nations." He must determine which method of ministry he will use to carry out this commission. As stated earlier, the pastor must know the people he shepherds; he must have awareness of the church's population and the community he services.

Chapter 2
Historical Review

Examination of the Church Decline

Much discussion and research concerning the issues of church decline have generated. Several articles and polling services like The Barna Group, The Pew Forum, and Gallup have presented information and statistics on church decline. Gallup has kept track of statistics on church decline dating back to 1948. An article by Jayson D. Bailey entitled *6 Important Church Attendance Statistics and What They Tell Us* reports that the Gallup poll relates a rise in "Nones". The "Nones" are people who do not attend a church. The poll says, "68 percent of people attended church in 1948; 71 percent in 1956 but [the number] dropped to 37 percent in 2016[13]". These statistics verify a steady church decline over the years, a problem that has been going on for some time. The church in the United States of America has work to do if it is going to stop and reverse the problem of decline or being stuck.

The Gallup poll posed a question about church attendance dating back to the 1950's. The question was, "Did you yourself happen to attend church?[14]" In 1950, 49 percent of respondents said they attended church weekly. However, in 2008 the number dropped to 42 percent and

---

[13] Jayson D. Bradley, 6 Important Church Attendance Statistics and What they Tell, Bellingham, WA

[14] Frank Newport, Church Leaders and Declining Religious Service Attendance, Gallup. September 2018

38 percent in 2017. This is another indication, as shown by the poll, that church attendance has declined. Notice this poll listed below:

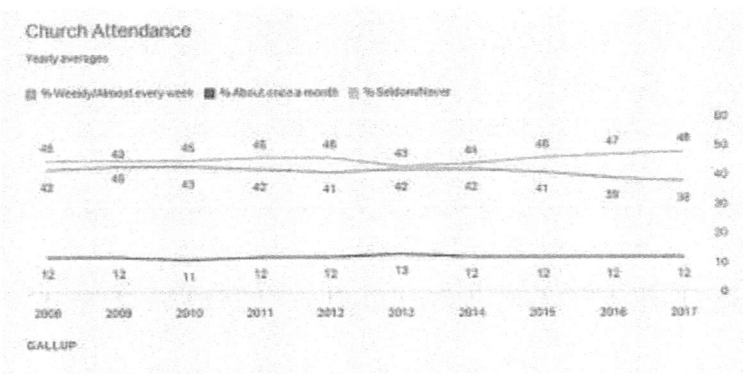

Thom S. Rainer conducted a research project on 1,000 churches from 2013 – 2016 to dispel the myth that 80 percent of churches in the United States of America were on the decline. The research project revealed some decline but not a decline as bad as reported. Rainer found that, "56 percent of churches are declining; 9 percent of churches are plateaued, and 35 percent of churches are growing[15]". It appears that 350 out of the 1,000 churches are growing while 650 churches are dead or stuck. In America, with the huge number of churches dead or stagnant, there is a need to help the 65 percent (dead and plateaued) experience growth like the 35 percent.

---

[15] Thom S. Rainer, Autopsy of the Church, B&H Publishing Group

An article in the *Baltimore Sun* written by Jonathan M. Pitts explains that churches are merging in the Maryland area because of decline issues. The writer spoke to the fact that because some churches are experiencing attendance stagnation and resultant rising maintenance costs, a decision to merge was a viable option. He reports, "The Episcopal Diocese of Maryland has closed a net of eight churches since 2007 and plans to close more[16]", Pitts also reports that the Delaware-Maryland Synod of the Evangelical Lutheran Church "consolidated eight of its small churches into three.[17]" He further reports that the African Methodist Episcopal Church "directed all 411 congregations in their jurisdiction to spend the next six months taking a hard look at their operations because of decline issues.[18]" This is a problem that is impacting all types churches an and communities across America.

The Barna Research group in its book entitled *Churchless* reported that only 49% of the adult population in the United States of America is actively churched. The "actively churched" refers to adults that have attended church regularly usually once a month or more. The problem is with the group defined as the "De-Churched," those adults who have attended church in the past but are currently on hiatus. The Barna Group says, "The De-Churched are the fastest growing segment, presently one-

---

[16] Johnathan M. Pitts, Churches merge, Close, Baltimore Sun, Oct. 2017

[17] Johnathan M. Pitts, Churches merge, Close, Baltimore Sun, Oct. 2017

[18] Johnathan M. Pitts, Churches merge, Close, Baltimore Sun, Oct. 2017

third of the population[19]". This group, representing 33 percent of the adult population, is contributing to the decline of the church. Some have said that the biggest door in the church is the back door. Churches must focus on closing the back door where people leave without going to another church. The Barna Group says, "The unchurched is becoming less responsive to the churches' efforts to connect with them.[20]" The group interviewed many people who were open to a friend inviting them to church; however, the church must find a way to inspire these individuals to stay. The church must discover or create an approach to reach this group if it is going to experience a turn-around.

Is Church Decline A Problem Today?

The problem of decline exists today and continues to be problem in many churches and denominations. During fellowships with churches from different denominations in the Southern New Jersey and Philadelphia areas, I have noticed over the years the problem of decline and have often mentioned these observations in conversations with the leaders of these churches. The churches are declining or stuck for many reasons; problems range from leadership to a membership who refuses to change. While some desire to grow, they resist a change in their ministry philosophy. They love the ministry but are afraid to

---

[19] George Barna & David Kinnaman, Churchless, Tyndale House Publishers, Inc

[20] George Barna & David Kinnaman, Churchless, Tyndale House Publishers, Inc

change what they have grown comfortable with even if it means staying stuck.

If we would focus on ten of these churches, seven are stuck or in decline. The pastors desire to be successful in ministry but the challenge to reverse the decline is too big for them to overcome. Several of these seven have pastors and leaders that are not strong enough in leadership, vision casting, or implementing a plan for growth. In addition, some pastors never trained their leaders in leadership and what it takes to lead. Moreover, some leaders rebelled against the pastors and refused to cooperate with their vision to move the church forward. They loved their past and were comfortable staying at that same position even if it met being stuck.

All seven churches lacked a commitment to evangelism and to carrying out the Great Commission found in Matthew 28:18 – 20: "Therefore, go and make disciples of all nations." If a church is not committed to evangelism and community missions, then it would be hard for it to grow and make an impact for the Kingdom of God. These churches lack vision and the ability to connect with their communities, and if these issues are not corrected, then these churches will eventually close.

Thom S. Rainer in his book *The Autopsy of the Church* mentioned some of these factors that I have observed in these seven declining or stuck churches. Rainer looked at fourteen churches and listed some of the reasons; they are the following: the past as their hero, a refusal to look like the community, budget issues, membership decline, pastoral issues, and a lack of prayer. He said, "Every one of the fourteen autopsied churches had some level of problem before they died.[21]" Churches do not die overnight. They show signs of issues and die overtime. These problems prevail today because churches are having a hard time trying to figure out how to address the death knell.

A Baptist Church Association in Southern New Jersey is one that I have familiarity with. This association, with over 50 churches in its membership, is being hit hard with church decline with many of its member churches facing the possibility of closure. The Association has not addressed the issue of being stuck and membership decline, and is instead ignoring the dilemma, giving very little conversation to the problem of decline. This Association had been strong twenty years ago but refused to change with the times and is now suffering a great loss. If this problem continues to be ignored, said association could see many of its churches close in the near future. There must be a conversation started soon so that this problem is addressed and resolved.

It should be noted that not all Baptist Churches in Southern New Jersey are stuck or in decline. Even so, church decline is impacting all denominations across New Jersey and the United States of America. The Baptist Resource Network (BRN) also has several churches in Southern New Jersey and Philadelphia areas that are

---

[21] Thom S. Rainer, Autopsy of the Church, B&H Publishing Group

declining, but, unlike the Baptist Association, the Southern Baptist Convention is addressing the decline issue through their Healthy Churches Department. The organization is putting together a plan to help churches in decline to reverse their problem. It has begun by meeting with pastors to start the discussion of correcting this problem before more churches are impacted by it.

What is needed for Revitalization?

The church decline problem is on the rise and appears to be unresolved today. It is a problem that now is starting to garner the attention of many pastors, conferences, church consultants, and church association groups. There are pastors in the Southern New Jersey and Philadelphia areas who want to start dialogue concerning church decline or being stuck. It appears that this problem has caught the church off guard, thereby, surprising the church with its impact on the church community in particular and denominations as a whole. A friend who serves as a bishop, recently informed me that several churches in Southern New Jersey have closed, and many more are stuck or in decline. He believes that too many churches in small rural areas have contributed to the decline in many churches. He further expressed that having even a hundred members in a congregation during this time is "really good."

Thom S. Rainer recently hosted a webinar presentation for pastors who are interested in becoming church consultants because of the problem with decline in the United States of America. These consultants will help assist churches with their problem of decline, working with them to turn this problem around. He believes churches are closing because of an inability of the individual churches to see health problems in their churches. Further, he believes churches are starting to see this problem but need help in reversing decline or the state of being stuck. Thom S. Rainer says there are deteriorating conditions in many of the churches in the United States of America with three-fourths of the nation's churches needing some type of intervention. This intervention would impact some 260,000 churches.

Dr. R A Vernon of the Word Church is holding a pastor and leadership conference in Cleveland, Ohio, on church decline. This conference named Change or Die is designed to help pastors and their leaders change from a declining church to a growing church. Evolving leadership is so important; as John Maxwell says in the *21 Irrefutable Laws of Leadership*, "Everything rises and falls on leadership.[22]" The greatest single factor in the success or failure of any church is leadership. The church needs leaders to be people of vision who spend time in prayer and in God's Word.

The Baptist Resource Network in the Philadelphia and Southern New Jersey areas oversees churches in those areas and is starting to address this problem of decline/stagnation among the churches in their

---

[22] John Maxwell, 21 Irrefutable Laws of Leadership, Thomas Nelson Publishers

organization. The Healthy Church department has put together a plan recently to address this problem. These days everyone seems to be health conscious; so, the church needs to be like the world in that regard, thinking about its health.

The Healthy Church Department recently held a Church Revitalization Conference with one of its seminars covering the topics of instruction of pastors and leaders on Biblical leadership, how to have a vision-driven church, and how to grow a church. Leadership is important for any church to move forward because since everything rises and falls with leadership, churches will suffer when there is poor leadership or none at all. Dr. Tony Evans says, "The church must take more seriously the Apostle Paul's admonition to prepare saints for the work of the ministry.[23]" If the work is being done, then the church will experience growth because disciples make disciples.

The Baptist Resource Network conference consisted of a panel of six pastors and leaders, of which I served as one. This panel was represented by thriving churches, some of which had been declining at one time. The attendees, other pastors, and leadership members asked questions of the panel regarding real life struggles and challenges ranging from declining churches to declining youth ministries. The discussion was fruitful with a decision to continue dialogue in the future with assistance for churches that requests help for decline.

---

[23] Dr. Tony Evans, Let's Get to Know Each Other, Thomas Nelson Publishers

A tool being used to start the revitalization of declining churches is the Church Health Assessment. This tool is being used by the Baptist Resource Network and other organizations to help churches to concentrate on areas of the ministry that are weak and causing decline. The Church Health Assessment can help declining churches to start on the road of becoming vibrant again. Rick Warren in an article entitled *Growth Is Okay, but Church Health Is What Matters* says, "Church health is the key to church growth.[24]" The church is a living organism which communicates that it is normal for it to grow. Living things grow, and if a church is not dead or declining, then it will experience the opposite of death or decline, which is growth. Similarly, the church is a body and not a company. Romans 12:4-5 reads, "For as we have many members in one body, and all members have not the same office. So, we are being many, are one body in Christ, and everyone members one of another." When parts of the body break down, intervention is needed to bring it back to health. Bodies need healing, not a shut down or a downsizing as companies do.

When the church is healthy and the body is working fitly together, then the church will see growth. Church growth is a result of church health. The SOAR Church prior to my arrival was a church that was divided by three families. This division was causing the church to decline because there was no focus on ministry or growth. As pastor, I

---

[24] Rick Warren, Growth is Okay, But Church Health is What Matters, Church Leaders.

came with a plan and a vision which consisted of leadership development, vision implementation, discipleship training, fellowship, worship, and community outreach, all of which revitalized the church. That plan was taken from the early church found in Acts 2:42-47, the early church that had the characteristics of a healthy church. Now, the early church in Acts 2 gave a healthy plan of fellowship, disciples, worship, ministry, and evangelism. These characteristics allowed addition to take place in the church which produced growth on a daily basis. In Acts 2:47, "The Lord added to the church daily such as should be saved." Rick Warren says, "When a church focuses on those healthy purposes, it will develop the healthy balance that make it grow[25]".

Therefore, starting with a Church Health Assessment could be the first step in helping churches to stop their decline and start a growth process. Several assessments are available for a church to utilize, such as, the one administered to Missouri Baptist Churches; their health assessment is called Show-Me Health. Similar to the check-ups for the human body, every church should take health assessments to make sure that areas of the ministry are not failing. Church decline can sneak up on a church very quickly, and just as assessments are given by other associations and organizations around the United States of America to point out strengths and weaknesses, churches should do likewise. Their assessment is based on the

---

[25] Rick Warren, Growth is Okay, But Church Health is What Matters, Church Leaders.

characteristics found in Acts 2:42-27. Please, note the health assessment listed below:

✝Evangelism is the faithful proclamation of Jesus Christ and Him crucified. The church is built through members being fervent in proclaiming Jesus Christ to a lost world. It is the responsibility of the local church to call all that would come to repentance and a new life in Jesus Christ. Romans 10:14-15 "How can they believe in the One of whom they have not heard?"

 # Evangelism Check-up

On a scale of 1 to 5 (1 being low; 5 being high), how would you rate your church in leading people to faith in the Lord Jesus Christ?

☐ 1. There is evidence that a majority of members share their faith with others and invite them to church.

☐ 2. Church emphasizes prayer for spiritually lost people to come to know Jesus as personal Savior and Lord.

☐ 3. Church has a system for greeting first time guest, receiving information from them, and helping them to feel welcome.

☐ 4. Church is organized and is training individuals in how to share their faith with others.

☐ 5. Church has a plan to identify guests and have members make a follow-up contact with them.

☐ 6. Members are often encouraged to identify people in their social network and to build relationships and share Christ with them.

☐ 7. Church plans and conducts regular outreach emphasis (e.g. special evangelistic events, servant evangelism projects, block parties, VBS, musical programs, etc.)

☐ 8. Church keeps and utilizes up-to-date prospect files.

☐ 9. Baptism is celebrated at least quarterly.

☐ 10. Church intentionally stays aware of the demographic make-up and needs within their community context and plans evangelistic strategies accordingly.

HEALTHY ZONE 40 to 50 points Overall good condition. Some Minor corrections could be made.

MARGINAL ZONE - 30 to 39 points Several changes in church lifestyle will need to be made.

UNHEALTHY ZONE -20 to 29 points. Resuscitation may be called for- STAT!

CRITICAL ZONE 10 to 19 points Emergency Surgery needs to be done to save this patient!

Total:_____

✝Fellowship is when believers share their lives with fellow believers. There is no believer that can live this Christian life in isolation. Acts 2:42 "They continued steadfastly in the apostles' doctrine and fellowship".

 # Fellowship Checkup

On a scale of 1 to 5 (1 being low; 5 being high), how would you rate your church in establishing and building relationships with God and His people?

☐ 1. Church teaches on and encourages believers to unite with the church through baptism or statement of faith.

☐ 2. Church has created an environment of belonging through grace, acceptance, support, and mutual encouragement.

☐ 3. Church provides opportunities to build relationships through fellowship activities beyond Sunday.

☐ 4. Church provides fellowship through Special Emphases such as Senior Adult Day, Student Day, etc., and/or holidays.

☐ 5. Church provides opportunities to build fellowship through praying and serving together.

☐ 6. Sunday School or small group maintains contact with members who are away from home & those in leadership in other age-groups.

☐ 7. There are regular sermons focusing on the significance of fellowship and living in community with other Christians.

☐ 8. Church has developed strategies for extending fellowship to those who are not part of the church.

☐ 9. Church is careful not to overburden staff members and volunteers so that they have time to build relationships.

☐ 10. Church leaders have been trained to handle conflicts constructively.

HEALTHY ZONE 40 to 50 points Overall good condition. Some Minor corrections could be made.

MARGINAL ZONE - 30 to 39 points Several changes in church lifestyle will need to be made.

UNHEALTHY ZONE -20 to 29 points. Resuscitation may be called for-STAT!

CRITICAL ZONE 10 to 19 points Emergency Surgery needs to be done to save this patient!

Total:_____

✝The church comes together to exalt the God. Worship is vital to the Christian life. A healthy church will come together regularly to worship God in ways that engage the believer's heart, mind, and strength. The early church worshipped God on a regular basis. Acts 2:47 "Praising God and having favour with all people." Also, Psalm 150, Psalm 86:9-10 and Psalm 100.

Worship Checkup

On a scale of 1 to 5 (1 being low; 5 being high), how would you rate your church in worship?

□ 1. Church acknowledges Jesus as Lord of all and responds by expressing love for him in worship.

□ 2. Church encourages/resources members to experience God's power/presence by seeking Him personally through daily prayers and devotion.

□ 3. Teachers establish an environment in Bible study classes that lead people to encounter the life-changing God.

□ 4. Church has examined how well its worship style and time(s) fits its members/prospective members, and has made changes where necessary.

□ 5. Church regularly involves volunteers in the worship service, both in planning, conducting, and evaluating.

□ 6. Church regularly involves volunteers in the worship service, both in planning, conducting, and evaluating.

□ 7. Worship leaders plan ahead and use a variety of creative elements in worship services such as readings, different styles of music, drama, video, sermons, etc.

□ 8. Church receives the offering as an act of worship.

□ 9. The Word of God is proclaimed faithfully and persuasively.

□ 10. Church services are designed to lead individuals to actively participate in corporate expressions of worship.

HEALTHY ZONE 40 to 50 points Overall good condition. Some Minor corrections could be made.

MARGINAL ZONE - 30 to 39 points Several changes in church lifestyle will need to be made.

UNHEALTHY ZONE -20 to 29 points. Resuscitation may be called for- STAT!

CRITICAL ZONE 10 to 19 points Emergency Surgery needs to be done to save this patient!

Total:_____

✝The church is commanded to make disciples. Disiciples are learners of Jesus Christ. A healthy church will be a place where people can come and learn about the Gospel of Jesus Christ. Matthew 28:19-20: "Go, ye, therefore, and teach all nations, baptizing them in the name of the Father, and of the Son and of the Holy Spirit. Teaching them to observe all things."

 # Sunday School/ Discipleship Checkup

On a scale of 1 to 5 (1 being low; 5 being high), how would you rate your church in Bible study and discipleship?

☐ 1. Pastor regularly emphasizes the importance of Sunday School/small groups and Discipleship from the pulpit.

☐ 2. Sunday School/small group and Discipleship leaders are enlisted early based on their spiritual gifts and are given appropriate training.

☐ 3. Sunday School leaders regularly attend planned workers meeting.

☐ 4. A new members class or group is made available.

☐ 5. Appropriate Bible study/Discipleship curriculum materials are provided for each age-group.

☐ 6. Church leadership has a clear Discipleship plan to help all believers mature in Christ.

☐ 7. Sunday School classes enroll new members regularly andare recognized for doing so.

☐ 8. Church encourages families to have a weekly "Family Bible Study" time together.

☐ 9. Church regularly starts new Sunday School classes or small groups.

☐ 10. Opportunities are provided throughout the year for doctrinal and special emphasis Bible studies.

HEALTHY ZONE 40 to 50 points Overall good condition. Some Minor corrections could be made.

MARGINAL ZONE - 30 to 39 points Several changes in church lifestyle will need to be made.

UNHEALTHY ZONE -20 to 29 points. Resuscitation may be called for- STAT!

CRITICAL ZONE 10 to 19 points Emergency Surgery needs to be done to save this patient!

Total:_____

✝The church is to serve those who are in need. Ministry is the vehicle where the church communicates the love of Jesus Christ to those outside also. Members should be challenged to carry out their calling through their God-given gifts. Romans 12:3-10, Ephesians 4:12: "For the perfecting of the saints, for the work of the ministry, for the edifying of the body of Christ."

 # Mission/ Ministry Checkup

On a scale of 1 to 5 (1 being low; 5 being high}, how would you rate your church in ministry/missions?

☐ 1. Church has a plan to identify and appropriately meet the benevolent needs within the congregation and community.

☐ 2. Church provides opportunities for church members to discover their gifts, talents and strengths; and a clear pathway to find ministries where they can be deployed.

☐ 3. Church is organized for effective ministry to members, prospects, and family members.

☐ 4. Church equips people for ministry/missions through ongoing Bible study and special training events.

☐ 5. Church involves individuals and groups in ministry/ missions through ministry projects, special assignments, and mission opportunities.

☐ 6. Church provides church wide ministry/missions projects for individuals and/or family participation.

☐ 7. Church demonstrates a climate open to ministry/missions in the local community and area.

☐ 8. Church demonstrates an openness to sponsor, aid, or participate in a new church start.

☐ 9. Church surveys the needs of members and non-members to determine future ministry goals.

☐ 10. Church body is regularly involved in missions education for all age groups.

HEALTHY ZONE 40 to 50 points Overall good condition. Some Minor corrections could be made.

MARGINAL ZONE - 30 to 39 points Several changes in church lifestyle will need to be made.

UNHEALTHY ZONE -20 to 29 points. Resuscitation may be called for- STAT!

CRITICAL ZONE 10 to 19 points Emergency Surgery needs to be done to save this patient!

Total:_____

 # Church Health Inventory "CHI"

In the spaces below, write the average score of all your church leadership team for each purpose. Subtotal the scores, then divide by seven to arrive at your total score. Use the thennometer to the right to see the overall health of your church. Spend time discussing each purpose and specif,c needs that show up on the checkup sheets. Then write the two top priorities you would like to work on in the coming months.

☐ EVANGELISM

1. _____

2. _____

☐ SUNDAY SCHOOL / DISCIPLESHIP

1. _____

2. _____

☐ FELLOWSHIP

1. _____

2. _____

☐ MINISTRY/ MISSIONS

1. _____

2. _____

☐ WORSHIP

1. _____

2. _____

☐ LEADERSHIP

1. _____

2. _____

☐ STEWARDSHIP

1. _____

2. _____

HEALTHY ZONE 40 to 50 points Overall good condition. Some Minor corrections could be made.

MARGINAL ZONE - 30 to 39 points Several changes in church lifestyle will need to be made.

UNHEALTHY ZONE -20 to 29 points. Resuscitation may be called for- STAT!

CRITICAL ZONE 10 to 19 points Emergency Surgery needs to be done to save this patient!

Total:_____

This book should help churches to focus on problem areas. The areas that are declining should be addressed through the power of prayer and the leading of the Holy Spirit. Without the leading of the Holy Spirit, it would be hard for church to turn around its decline.

What is the impact of the Church Decline?

Many have seen churches that used to be vibrant now in serious decline in the Southern New Jersey area. Several churches within miles of each other were thriving and relevant twenty years ago but have now declined and are on the verge of closing. At least seven out of ten churches in this small county within the ten-mile radius have an average of twenty to forty people in weekly attendance, and two of these churches are on the verge of closing within the year.

This problem of decline has impacted these churches with a loss of membership. People are no longer interested in attending these churches, and because of this, their reputation in the county has caused them to be referred to as dead churches. The lack of membership has put a serious strain on these churches financially. Because of a lack of finances, it has become hard to maintain their buildings, buildings that used to be beautiful places now in decay and falling down. There is a smell of death when you enter into the building, a smell of death in a building that does not look clean, a building with physical evidence of walls falling, and a building with fixtures no longer working. These are sad sights of places that used to play a vital role in their communities.

There is little to no evangelism taking places in these churches. A church cannot grow without reaching the community through evangelism. When there is no evangelism, there will be no Gospel being presented to a lost world. Because of a lack of growth and disappearance of evangelism, most of these churches are run by people in their seventies. Two of the churches have pastors in their 90's. These are churches where pastors who have stayed too long and have contributed to the decline of the church because vision is no longer in effect.

These churches have no future because there is an absence of family and youth. A young generation is needed so that the church can have a future; when there is an absence of a younger generation, it will be hard for the church to move forward. These churches are also trying to survive off the income of seniors who are on fixed incomes. These stories are being played out in local churches, in churches in this county, and all over the United States of America. There are similar stories in the urban area of Philadelphia, Pennsylvania., one of which involves a pastor housed in a huge church building with twenty members, mostly seniors who have been in that church for many years. Sadly, in the ten years this pastor has been pastor there, it has not grown. This pastor expressed how hard it has been to keep the building open. Decline or the state of being stuck does not have compassion on any building or congregation. It is closing ministries and buildings at a fast rate.

In Bill Henard's book entitled *Reclaimed Church: How Churches Grow, Decline and Experience Revitalization* the author agrees with Thom S. Rainer's assessment of church decline. He believes that there is a church decline problem in the United States of America and "400,000 churches in the United States are declining or have plateaued.[26]" He noted similar problems with declining churches that were seen in a small county in Southern New Jersey and in Philadelphia. Some of the impacts that he observed were that people were no longer attending, that people were less engaged, that leaders were leaving, that money was no longer coming in, that members had grown old, that key staff was lost, that weak leadership team was evident, and that no evangelism was occurring.

Churches need to change if they are going to turn around this problem of decline or stagnation. Many churches are slow to change while the face of culture and emergence of technology are changing everything. If churches are going to start revitalization, they must embrace change. There are many churches in the United States of America that are growing, some of which used to be in decline but started a revitalization that initiated a growth process. The SOAR Church is the picture of a church that embraced both a God-led vision and change. It started a revitalization process that, in turn, started growth. Bill Henard says, "Churches and businesses that embrace change and development and market strategies that engage

---

[26] Bill Henard, Reclaimed Church, B&H Publishing Group, Nashville, TN

these changing landscapes are reaching their target groups[27]".

There are many churches that have changed their methods but not their message, and that change has resulted in growth and vibrancy in today's society. Most of these churches have adopted similar characteristics reflective of today's culture, such as, shorter services, dress-down approach, worship teams, praise dances, relevant messages that address the needs of today, theater lights, stages, and strong presence of technology and social media. Quentin J. Schultze writes in his book *High-Tech Worship* says, "In our worship, too, we cannot escape technologies. Digital technology is simply a part of life for most people.[28]" The church needs to understand that technology is not a curse but could be a blessing to help further the Kingdom of God. Social media could be used as modern-day evangelism. Many churches that are vibrant use social media to broadcast their services and to spread the gospel message. If the world uses social media to broadcast up-to-the-minute news, what prevents the church from using it to spread the gospel message to an entire world that is using that platform? Change is necessary if the church is going to be relevant in today's society.

---

[27] Bill Henard, Reclaimed Church, B&H Publishing Group, Nashville, TN

[28] Quentin J. Schultze, High-Tech Worship, Baker Book, Grand Rapids, MI

Chapter 3
Practical Application

The Church Can Live

Many churches, associations, conferences, and organizations are starting to address the problem of decline or stagnation. The problem of being stagnant or in decline is being addressed through health assessments, church consultant groups, seminars, conferences, and books on the subject. Although the problems of decline and stagnation have been around for a long time, they are now garnering the attention they need because of the impact on the Kingdom of God. If a church is dealing with the problem of decline and desires to address this problem, there are resources available such as those mentioned. The key to revitalization starts with the individual churches and their desire to "fix" the condition. In fixing it, there is a change that must take place, but many churches are stuck or in decline because they refuse to change. The message never needs to change but the approach and methods of doing ministry must change. In order to achieve revitalization, these churches must explore the benefits of conferences, seminars, webinars, church consultant groups, training, and books that will help the church to become effective during this time. Ed Stetzer and Thom S. Rainer talked about the importance of change in their book *Transformational Church*. Everyday people are confronted with change as a society; there are new developments every day. The authors stated, "No matter what we do, change comes to all of us.[29]" In other words, change has the ability to find people on a daily basis no matter what their station in life. For example, people do not dress the way they did twenty years ago, nor do they drive the types of cars from two decades ago. Telephones have immensely changed in appearance and functionality from twenty years prior; yet the device continues to be extremely popular and excessive in cost. Even television viewing has undergone dramatic technological advances offering a different viewer format from twenty years ago. It is amazing that people and their "toys" change with the times, but, nostalgically and legalistically, they want the church to remain as it was decades ago and not change with the times. Ed Stetzer and Thom S. Rainer relate, "We can't choose whether change will come or not. But we can choose whether to embrace it or resist it[30]". So many churches stuck in the past resist change today, but they must become educated in the importance of change if church decline is going to be arrested and revitalization is going to take place.

There must be a connection with today's society if churches are going to reach the lost for Jesus Christ. A connection with those who currently attend church services must be maintained so that these congregants will continue to attend, to grow, and to invite others. A change

---

[29] Ed Stetzer and Thom S. Rainer, Transformational Church. B&H Publishing Group.

[30] Ed Stetzer and Thom S. Rainer, Transformational Church. B&H Publishing Group.

is necessary so that the church can be relevant in connecting with those it is supposed to impact. Ryan Sheehan, writer for the *Christian Post,* relates about individuals leaving the church because they do not feel connected. He says, "There is an ongoing silent migration away from the church of an estimated 3,500 individuals on a daily basis[31]". Although his research was done in 2015, Sheehan believes that migration continues today and that it has contributed to the decline of the church. The church must make modifications in order to correct its connection problem with people so that the state of decline and the migration of individuals leaving the church will cease. The church must understand what it takes to connect with individuals today, and there are churches experiencing growth today because of their understanding of the importance of connecting with people. The WORD Church in Cleveland, OH; Elevation Church in Charlotte, NC; Life Church in Edmond, OK; ENON Tabernacle Baptist Church in Philadelphia, PA; Delaware Valley Baptist Church in Willingboro, NJ; North Point Church in Alpharetta, GA, and The SOAR Church in Woodbine, NJ, are some that understand what it means to be relevant in their ministry approach, teaching, preaching, and outreach.

The SOAR Church of Woodbine, NJ, is a church that had been stuck in a no-growth situation. It was in decline because of several issues but has since turned around through revitalization and is now growing. Changing its methods of delivery but not the message was the action

---

[31] Ryan Sheehan, The Christin Post

plan The SOAR Church used to address its decline. The plan that SOAR instituted is a plan that can be used by other churches that are stuck or in decline. With the intention to assist other churches,

SOAR is sharing its plan with several churches from the Philadelphia and Southern New Jersey areas at its yearly training, SOAR Leadership Academy. This training includes topics on growing ministry, developing leadership, and reaching community for Jesus Christ. The hope is that The SOAR Church can help declining churches reverse their trend by applying some of the processes and plans that SOAR has used. Processes and plans do not discriminate and can be adapted and applied to many churches that are stuck or in decline. My prayer is that this plan can help churches around the United States of America with their problem of being stagnant or in decline. A church in the Philadelphia area followed this plan and is no longer stuck but is connecting with their community and is experiencing growth numerically and spiritually.

The SOAR Church's building blocks to turning around decline consisted of Prayer, Vision Casting, Leadership Development, Develop a Creating Team, and Outreach.

SOAR Church Building Blocks to Turning Around the Conditions of Church Decline and Stagnation

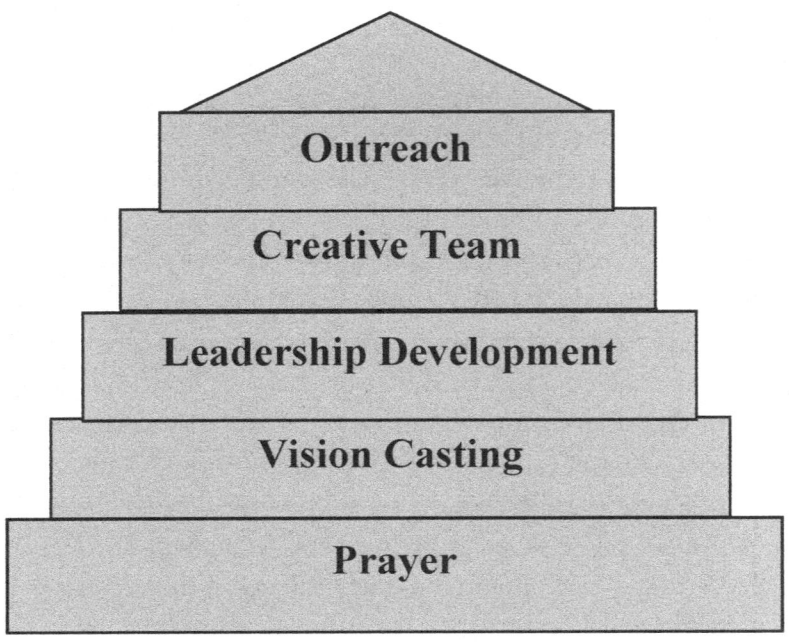

Prayer

Prayer is the foundation of The SOAR Church's implementation process to turn around its decline. It was the key that helped to start the process of reversing its decline. The SOAR Church's leadership and membership would pray collectively on Saturday mornings, seeking God's direction for the church. This prayer is now done every weekday morning from 7:00 am to 7:10 am on social media platforms averaging 300 people daily. Once growth has been established, praying for the ministry and for direction should never stop. Prayer is essential because trying to turn around declining or stuck churches comes with opposition. Anytime a church wants to make an impact for the Kingdom of God, there will be problems and challenges. The SOAR Church experienced internal conflict between members, death threats on the pastor's life, and a loss of members who did not like change. Moreover, prayer was needed to help the faithful to move forward and to stand in the midst of attacks. The concept of change can be hard to accept for some; so, prayer is the tool to help the faithful followers to get through to process of turning around church decline.

When a church is about to implement a plan to correct any problem, prayer must be the foundational element. Praying and then planning should go hand in hand. After a health assessment is done and weak areas are revealed, churches should take those areas in prayer to God for His direction. Prayer, one part of which is talking to God, our Creator, who knows everything about us, is vital for the church, and listening for His answer, the other part of prayer, is the necessary component to get direction. It is hard for any church to move forward or turn around its decline if it is not praying. Prayer will help the church clearly see the vision and direction that God has mapped out for it.

Nehemiah saw the condition of the ruined and dilapidated walls in Jerusalem and wanted to do something about it. Nehemiah prayed about what he saw and sought God for direction. Nehemiah was not free to act upon what he saw because he was cup bearer (food taster) for the king, and as a servant in captivity, he had no authority to act upon his desire. Prayer moved the king; it can move on individuals to give favor today. Nehemiah 1:11: "O Lord, I beseech Thee, let now Thine ear be attentive to the prayer of Thy servant, and to the prayer of Thy servants, who desire to fear Thy name: and prosper, I pray Thee, Thy servant this day, and grant him mercy in the sight of this man. For I was the king's cupbearer." Nehemiah's prayer opened the door for God to move on the king's heart thus allowing Nehemiah to share the vision with king. He is then allowed to move forward with the vision to repair the broken walls and given authority by the king to fix the problem. Prayer can move obstacles that may be standing in the way of a church trying to move forward.

Nehemiah never prayed for God to rebuild the wall but for an opportunity to rebuild it. In addition, Nehemiah prayed for success and God granted him what he prayed about, opportunity and success. So, if the church would pray about vision and direction concerning revitalizing churches that are stuck or in decline, God will send opportunities to correct this problem because the church is God's creation and design, and He is invested in their success. Prayer is critical for any church to move forward in revitalization.

Vision Casting

The SOAR Church would not be what it is today without a vision and without the membership's understanding of the vision and running with it. Vision is vital for any ministry to move forward, and if a church is going to turn around its decline and its stagnation, it must have a God-given vision. Proverbs 29:18: "Where there is no vision the people are restrained." The absence of a vision will hinder the church from moving. After talking to several pastors in the Southern New Jersey and Philadelphia areas, I discovered that there were very few pastors whose churches had a vision in place. A church will decline when there is a lack of vision while a church with a vision will help its membership turn in God's directions. James E. Means in his book *Effective Pastors for a New Century* says, "Thousands of pastors simply do not know how to get their churches moving or how to penetrate their communities with the Gospel message.[32]" In my conversations with these pastors recently, it appeared that there is a sense of loss concerning what vision is. A deacon recently told me that he was content being a traditional church with just fifteen members. This same deacon is a leader in a church with a new pastor who is trying to implement and cast vision, but the membership is rejecting it and comfortable with decline.

Philip Greenslade in his book *Leadership, Greatness and Servanthood* says, "To say, 'I have no vision for this church' is the saddest thing any pastor can say.[33]" Vision carries a sense of conviction, a conviction to help people. The SOAR Church has a conviction to help families of autistic children. As a result, The SOAR Church raises

---

[32] James E. Means. Effective Pastors for a New Century. Grand Rapids. Baker Books

[33] Philip Greenslade. Leadership, Greatness and Servanthood. Minneapolis. MN. Bethany Publishers.

thousands of dollars a year that is donated to local schools to support their special needs classes. This conviction has allowed the SOAR Church to donate over $40,000 to local schools over the past five years. The conviction of vision begins with the decision not to accept things the way they are. Vision says, "I see an issue and I'm going to do something about it." Churches need a vision for their particular community where God has placed them, a God-given vision unique to each church and to the needs of those surrounding the church.

Every church should have a vision that is unique to its ministry. Vision will help the church to know who it is, what it stands for, where it is going, and how it is to get there; it serves as a road map for that congregation. If there is no vision, then the church will be lost, and decline will begin to set in. Andy Stanley in his book *Visioneering* says, "All divinely inspired visions are in some way tied into God's master plan.[34]" God works behind the scenes putting things in place to move the ministry forward. He says, "God is using your circumstances to prepare you to accomplish His vision for your life.' Vision is not easy, but it is necessary for church growth. It will be hard for any church to grow where there is no vision.

The vision must be cast before the membership on a regular basis if they are going to run with it. Habakkuk 2:2: "And the Lord answered me, and said, "Write the vision, make it plain upon tables, that he may run that

---

[34] Andy Stanley. Visioneering. Multnomah Publishers: 1999

readeth it." Habakkuk was encouraged by God to write a vision so that people could read it and then execute it. Similarly, today, the vision must be written out so that the membership can read it, understand it, and run with it. Every church should have a vision that is visible, taught, and understood. If companies have their vision statements on the walls for the workers to see, why should the church not do the same. Companies will make sure that their employees know the vision and understand their mission, their responsibility, and their benefit in the mission and vision. The SOAR Church communicates the vision to its members on a regular basis. Whatever ministries the church has and whatever ministries its members are engaged in, it is imperative that they line up with SOAR's vision of Reaching, Reproducing, Reclaiming, and Rebuilding. They reach the lost, reproduce by making disciples, reclaim those who are lost or falling away, and rebuild those who are broken.

Vision must be cast at the appropriate time to the appropriate people. It will always seem impossible. There were times during vision implementation at The SOAR Church when vision seemed impossible and growth seemed as if it would never happen. The SOAR Church's vision was crafted in the year 2000 but did not get started until the year 2008. Habakkuk 2:3 "For the vision is yet for an appointed time, but in the end it shall speak." The right people had to be in place for the vision to come into pass. Vision and church growth take time and patience.

Leadership Development

The pastor cannot grow a church by himself. He needs leaders who will work alongside him to help implement the vision that God has given to the church. One reason many churches suffer decline or stagnation is the issue of constant conflict between the pastor and leadership. Carey Nieuwhof in his book "*Lasting Impact, 7 Powerful Conversations that Will Help your Church Grow*" noted that one of the causes of decline is conflict among the leadership. He wrote that "Internal dysfunction that is sapping the community of its life, such as conflict.[35]" When a church has constant conflict, it will destroy the unity not only in leadership but within the entire church. Church conflict will definitely cause a church to decline because people do not want to be part of a church that has conflict on a consistent basis. Carey Nieuwhof advises, "Growing churches handle conflict directly, biblically, humbly and healthy.[36]"

I know of a pastor, who after only ten months on the job, resigned because of daily conflict with leadership. Another pastor has been on the job for two years, but the church has not installed him as pastor because of two deacons who have not only rejected vision and change but also have plotted constantly to get rid of him. The in-

---

[35] Neiuwhof, Carey, Lasting Impact "7 Powerful Conversations that will help your church grow", The Rethink Group, Cumming, GA.

[36] Neiuwhof, Carey, Lasting Impact "7 Powerful Conversations that will help your church grow", The Rethink Group, Cumming, GA.

fighting has been going for two years; the results, church decline, no ministry, and no growth. If they stay that course, the pastor will leave, and the church will be in jeopardy of closing. These churches were offered help with their problems, but leadership continues to reject it. Both churches have approximately thirty members total with two strong personalities in each church controlling the entire church. If a church is going to turn around its decline, the pastor and leadership must work together.

The church needs leaders that are healthy spiritually. Healthy leaders can help the church to become healthy as a whole because, as simple as it sounds, healthy leaders create healthy churches. Such a simplistic statement holds overwhelming truth. A healthy leadership will spread throughout the congregation because healthy attitudes and lifestyles become contagious. When one characterizes a healthy leader, such characterization communicates an individual that is spiritually, emotionally, relationally, and physically healthy. Leaders can be given health assessments to see if there are areas of their lives that they need to address to make them healthy. Since the leadership is comprised of individuals and/or teams that work with the volunteers doing ministry for the church, health in the aforementioned areas is paramount. If there are problems and unhealthiness on the leadership level, then the volunteers will not be able to perform their jobs effectively.

Consequently, it is important for churches to develop and train leaders on a consistent basis. A church will not grow if the leadership is stagnant, ineffective, or uninformed. To that end, The SOAR Church has leadership training on a monthly basis; training includes spiritual leadership, how to do ministry, teamwork, vision casting, outreach, discipleship, and importance of spiritual growth. The leadership oversees the ministries of fellowship, worship, discipleship, and outreach, all based on Acts 2:41-47. If the leadership is not effective, then those areas of ministry will suffer and a decline in membership could occur.

A healthy leadership will come together and develop a strategy for growth. Church does not stop at the vision level; there must be a strategy developed by the leadership on how it will carry out the vision. Carey Nieuwhof says, "Growing churches develop a carefully thought-out strategy.[37]" One can have a clear vision but if there is no strategy for growth or ministry then the church will remain stuck or in decline. A church should always be thinking, *"What's the Next Big Thing?"* In The SOAR Church after one event is executed, the leadership will always look to do The Next Big Thing. Getting stuck on past successes will cause the church to be stuck in the past. For example, The Autism Awareness Walk done in April raises over $10,000 annually for the local schools. The SOAR Church invites the entire community to be part of their Autism Walk. Jesus Christ in Matthew 9:9 "As Jesus was walking along, He saw a man named Matthew sitting at his tax

---

[37] Neiuwhof, Carey, Lasting Impact "7 Powerful Conversations that will help your church grow", The Rethink Group, Cumming, GA.

collector's booth. Follow Me and be My disciple." Jesus gave Matthew a simple invitation that changed his life. The SOAR Church has seen people come to Christ because of invitations to individuals to join in and contribute to Autism Awareness.

Leaders learn to celebrate events and then move on to the next event. They do not linger on that event. When leaders have a strategy, they will always know what the next event will be. For example, the next event after the annual Autism Awareness Walk would be SOAR's pizza lunch supplied to the local school that works with special needs students. The lunch will consist of 45 free large pizzas for the students. Leadership should always be looking for "the next big thing" so that the ministry stays fresh and exciting for people. A strategy can look like the following diagram listed:

Year 2019	Leadership Training	Fellowship	Worship	Discipleship	Outreach
1st Quarter	Vision	Marriage	Develop social media presentation	Follow-up on new members	Coat Giveaway
2nd Quarter	Teamwork		Review worship songs	Closing the back door	Community Connections
3rd Quarter	Communication	Picnic	Train worship leaders.	Review new members classes	School Supplies
4th Quarter	Assessment	Christmas fellowship			Outreach to Schools

Creative Team

Creativity is something that is needed in churches today. Churches need to be creative by thinking outside the box in order to reach this generation. It is a generation driven by information and social media. Churches must change their methods but not the message in order to reach a generation that is constantly processing information. Quentin Schultze, in his book *High-Tech* [38][39]" If we are living in a technological society where information is distributed on a minute-by-minute basis, then the church has to get creative on how to use technology to its advantage.

There are many churches that have become creative and proficient in the use social media to market their ministries, promote the Gospel, and broadcast their services. The SOAR Church uses social media every day to broadcast its weekly prayer call which has grown because of social media, to broadcast its Sunday services which have increased in membership because of viewership, and to present messages about the Gospel which allows SOAR to reach the lost around the world. Promoting and presenting the gospel on social media is free; it costs nothing to join. The SOAR Church views the

---

[38] ,Schultze, Quentin. High-Tech Worship? "Using Presentational Technologies Wisely." Grand Rapids, MI. Baker Books

[39] [39] Schultze, Quentin. High-Tech Worship? "Using Presentational Technologies Wisely." Grand Rapids, MI. Baker Books

use of social media as modern-day evangelism as there has been a shift from going door to door with the Gospel to using social media as the new door-to- door. It reaches many quicker and covers more ground. Creativity will help churches to use social media to their advantage.

Ed Young, Jr., in his book *The Creative Leader,* talks about the importance of creativity in ministry. Young, who has been very creative with his sermons and ministry approach, recently built a basketball court on the stage to do a series on March Madness. He believes that creativity has caused his leaders and church to grow. He states, "The creative leader understands the past, lives in the present, and anticipates the future.[40]" The creative leader does not react but is proactive. Creativity will empower churches to understand where they are moving into the future.

Young believes that creativity will energize leaders and mobilize volunteers. People do not like to follow a vision that is stagnant or dead. Creativity will give the vision and the people life. The SOAR Church has seen members get excited and energized when creativity has been added to ministry events. The creativity team at The SOAR Church successfully sought out the Philadelphia Eagles, New York Giants, New York Jets, and Mike Trout of the California Angels to send items to be given away for Autism Awareness; this created an excitement among the people.

---

[40] Young, Ed. The Creative Leader: Unleashing the Power of your Creative Potential. Nashville, TN: Broadman & Holman Publishers

The SOAR Church has a creative team who assist leaders in developing creative ideas in doing ministry. For example, a creative arts ministry was developed which consisted of drama, dance, and mentoring for the youth ministry. This creative arts ministry attracts young people to the church because these are activities that they can relate to. One of the tasks the creative team is assigned includes developing ideas for the school supply giveaway. It has also been significant in developing changes to worship services through welcoming teams that create and foster a welcoming environment. Creativity, or thinking out of the box, is needed if the church is going to grow in today's world.

Outreach

Every church should have a desire to make an impact on the community where God has planted it. Many churches are stuck in their buildings and are reluctant to reach outside the building. The church is a living organism and must go outside in order to spread the Gospel of Jesus Christ to those who are lost. Luke 19:10 "For the Son of Man is come to seek and to save that which is lost." Sadly, there are churches in Southern New Jersey that have little to no outreach taking place. How can a church grow if it is not trying to reach those who are lost? The lost do not always find their way to the church; it is the charge of believers to go out and compel the lost, the backslider, and the inconsistent to come. Outreach must be a big part of any vision a church has today. Too many churches are inward focused and not outward focused.

The SOAR Church's outreach effectiveness in its community is due in part to its philosophy that the church should reflect and serve its community. The membership of SOAR Church is multi-cultural mirroring the community where it is placed and has developed an outreach plan designed to meet the needs of that community. Matthew 25:35 – 36 "For I was a hungered, and ye gave me meat, I was thirsty, and ye gave me drink: I was a stranger, and ye took me in. Naked and ye clothed me: I was sick and ye visited me: I was in prison, and ye came unto me." The SOAR Church uses this scripture as its guide. The church gives away coats in the winter and school supplies in the summer, feeds hungry families monthly, works with local law enforcement officers on issues of safety, records, and employment opportunities, engages with local colleges to introduce programs and inspire students to attend, works with local agencies to do ministry in the community, and partners with FBI Community outreach to provide information, promote safety and awareness of dangers to youth. All these resources have opened avenues for the SOAR Church to connect with the community; these connections have grown the church as a result. People want to be part of a church that is helping them during times of need.

Every church should be focused on meeting the needs of its community. The Bible has commissioned the church to do so. Churches across the United States that are meeting the needs of their communities and are connected to their communities are experiencing growth. The WORD Church in Cleveland, OH, gives to the local schools, to communities and to those in need, and, as a result, the church has been blessed. The church cannot stay inside and expect to grow without ever reaching those on the outside. There must be a plan for community outreach for the church to grow and avoid a decline.

This is just one plan that can be used to address the problem of decline that is impacting churches and communities across this the United States of America. Though the plan is not perfect, it has helped to turn around a church that was stuck and on the verge of decline. There are many plans available through churches and conferences, but it is the individual church's responsibility to reach out for help to stop decline and start revitalization.

Action Needed to Fix Church Decline

Thom S. Rainer recently did a presentation concerning how to help declining churches. This presentation was designed to recruit individuals who would help churches solve this problem by becoming consultants. He explained that consultants are needed to address this problem because of the high number of churches that are in decline. In fact, Rainer stated there are more churches in decline than consultants to help with the problem. His presentation charted three-fourths of the churches in United States of America - 260,000 - are in deteriorating conditions. These are churches needing intervention before they see themselves closing. He has a consultant university that has fewer than 200 functional consultants to deal with declining churches but is in need of more.

Church consultants are needed because most denominations and organizations do not have the budgets nor staff to deal with the numerous churches experiencing decline. Thom S, Rainer was trying to address this condition by recruiting more church consultants that would help alleviate the problems. Churches need people with experience who will come alongside leaders and members and help them deal with this problem that is spreading at so rapid a pace.

The Baptist Resource Network of Philadelphia and New Jersey has developed a plan to deal with declining churches. This organization is in the process of meeting with all their area churches, those that are in decline and those that are healthy. Their goal is to find a way for the healthy churches to help the declining churches because there are more declining churches than there are healthy ones. In addition, there is a seminar set up in the fall of 2019 to address this problem with the Southern New Jersey churches. Offerings include teachings on revitalization and a panel from healthy churches that will address the issues of the declining churches. This is just part of an ongoing process designed to turn around declining churches and get ahead of the problem before it gets worse.

Several books are available that address this problem. Thom S. Rainer's popular book the *Autopsy of a Decreased Church* communicates 12 ways to keep your church alive. Tony Morgan has a book *Stuck in a Funk?* which speak to how to get your church moving forward. Tony Morgan also has a book *The Unstuck Church,* which will equip churches to experience sustained health. Bill Henard's book *Reclaimed Church* details how churches Grow, Decline and Experience Revitalization.

Conferences are being started that deal with this issue. If a church wants to turn around and experience revitalization, there are many resources available and groups offering help so the problem can be addressed and remedied. This is not an individual church problem, but a problem that impacts the entire Body of Christ. If many churches are not growing, then the Kingdom of God is not winning souls and carrying out the Great Commission found in Matthew 28:18-20.

Strategies for Growth

This book has presented health assessments, plans, and processes that churches can use to move from decline to revitalization. After churches have done an assessment, they should put a plan and process in place to move from decline to revitalization; then a strategy is needed to start the process. Growing churches have a vision, a plan, and a strategy to help the church to accomplish its vision. Plan your work then work your plan through a strategy, a strategy for growth from healthy churches for declining churches. Churches need to ask the following: What strategy is needed for vision? What strategy is needed to put a halt to decline and restart growth? What is needed to engage people for the next season of growth? What structure is needed for growth to take place? What change is needed in order to restart growth? These questions can help a church to develop a strategy for growth.

Listed below are some strategies that can be used to help a church to stop its decline and restart growth. The SOAR Church has used some of these strategies and they helped to restart the church and lead them into a season of growth:

Make the Decision to Grow

In reality, some churches that are stuck in the past do not want to experience growth. Thom S. Rainer reported that in some of the churches that he had performed "autopsies" on, it revealed felt the past was their hero. He said, "They were fighting for the past.[41]" When a church fights for the past, there will be little desire to change and grow. If a church is going to grow, there must be a decision and a motivation from the leadership and members to want to grow.

When I was asked to pastor The SOAR Church, there were many in leadership that desired to grow the church. They were tired of being stuck while other churches around them were experiencing growth. So, after praying and seeking God's face, they selected the pastor that they believed would take them into a season of growth. A church must be motivated to stop its decline and grow the church. A church cannot move on from decline if it is not motivated to move toward a season of growth.

The Lord honors movement. When a church moves, God goes before them and opens up necessary doors that are

---

[41] Thom S. Rainer, Autopsy of the Church, B&H Publishing Group

needed for the journey. It was hard for the Nation of Israel to take the Promise Land without being motived to move. Notice what God told Joshua and the people in Joshua 1:9-10 "Have not I commanded thee? Be strong and of good courage; be not afraid neither be thou dismayed: for the Lord thy God is with thee whithersoever thou goest. Then Joshua commanded the officers of the people saying, Ye shall pass over this Jordan to go in possess the land." God honored their movement. If a church is going to start its revitalization, then it must be motivated to move from being stuck.

Know Where the Church Is Going

If you fail to plan, you plan to fail. It is vital that every member is oriented and educated on the vision to move forward. The vision must be able to reach the back row of the church. Members should be able to communicate a well-defined vision to the entire church so that everyone knows where the church is going. A vision maps out the necessary steps to get where the church is headed and how the vision will be achieved. Proverb 29:18 "Where there is no vision, the people perish."

People will be drawn to a vision that is compelling and they will get excited about it. People are inspired when they are challenged to do great things. Andy Stanley says, "vision-driven people are motivated people.[42]" People are motivated when they know where they are going because it gives meaning to life. The membership needs to know

---

[42] Andy Stanley. Visioneering. Multnomah Publishers: 1999

what is important, and when the direction is clearly spelled out, it helps people to see and understand what is important.

Identify Leaders and Train Them

Carey Nieuwhof says, "Churches that fail to release high-capacity leaders will struggle with growth."[43] The church must be able to identity people who are gifted to lead; gifted leaders will help the church to advance in its mission. At the SOAR Church members are given spiritual gifts survey. This survey both helps the members to identify and understand the area of their giftedness and helps the church to identify leaders and where they can serve. Too many times the church will have people in leadership positions because they have been in the church for a long time. Longevity should not be a qualification for leadership.

True leaders will create momentum where they serve and demonstrate the ability to get others to follow them. Carey Nieuwhof explains how to know a real leader. He says, "Check to see if anyone's following them. Second, look for Godly people who have a track record of handling responsibility in other areas of life humbly but capably.[44]" When you identify persons with true leadership skills, it is

---

[43] Neiuwhof, Carey, Lasting Impact "7 Powerful Conversations that will help your church grow", The Rethink Group, Cumming, GA.

[44] Neiuwhof, Carey, Lasting Impact "7 Powerful Conversations that will help your church grow", The Rethink Group, Cumming, GA.

important to start training those individuals and then give them a job of helping to lead the church into the future. The church must provide individuals with the opportunity to serve. Raising up future leaders will help the church not to stumble with growth issues in the future.

Create an Inviting Atmosphere

The church must create an atmosphere where people feel welcomed. If your church is going to turn around its decline or its stagnation, it must make people who visit feel welcomed. When people visit a particular church, they may be asking themselves. "Is this the church for me and my family?" If they can answer these questions quickly, it will be better for that church. At the SOAR Church, the First Touch Team, which consists of parking attendants, greeters at the front door and in the hallway, and ushers in the worship center, are charged with creating the first welcoming environment visitors and members see. They are called First Touch also because they are the ones people will come into contact with at the SOAR Center. In addition to those duties, The First Touch ministry is to connect with visitors as soon as possible. In general, churches have only one opportunity to make an impression on people.

Creating an inviting atmosphere is making sure there is not a smell of death in your church. A smell of death conveys death, decline, and stagnation in its physical appearance, for example, lack of cleanliness, unclean odor, old carpet, dim lighting, broken pews, and no excitement about Jesus Christ. People like to be proud about attending a church that is alive and full of excitement and passion.

Reach Out to New People

The church cannot grow if it does not know how to reach people. There must be a strategy to reach the lost if the church is going to grow and not be stuck. Growing churches know how to Get People, Keep People, and Grow People. They Get People by creating a strategy to reach people. They will design a way to create traffic into their worship services; a church cannot grow or turn around its decline if no people are coming to its services. A growing church will create ministries, produce creative sermons, hold outreach events, and develop ideas to bring people into the church. These churches will have ideas like Each One Reach One and Bring One Sundays just to create traffic into the church,

Growing churches know how to Keep the People they reach. The church must have a plan to get people involved in the ministry. People are busy in the world and need to be busy when they come into the church. Growing churches keep people by providing them with opportunities to serve. People will conform when there are expectations upon their lives.

Growing churches know how to Grow People. The church should know how to make disciples, or learners of Jesus Christ. When growing churches teach people to be like Jesus Christ, they are engaging people to make an impact for the Kingdom of God. Their engagement will help to advance the King of God.

Grow your Social Media Presence

The church can market a free sample of their ministry by promoting their ministry on social media. A church service can allow onlookers to experience their services in real time. Some growing churches are using social media to give people a glimpse of what they have to offer, using social media as an evangelism tool to attract people to their ministries. Social media also provides an opportunity for the church to share events and demonstrate how God is working in the lives of people.

Social Media is a place where the entire world connects and engages each other. It is an avenue of media where the presence the Gospel can be taught, shared, and illuminated because social media provide outlets where everyone hangs out. It gives the church an opportunity to engage people who would not necessarily walk-through church doors on a Sunday morning. A growing church will work to get the entire church involved in their social media strategy. At the SOAR Church, the members work very hard on social media to share all the church's information. The morning prayer call is shared; weekly services are shared, and ministry events are shared by the members on their personal accounts. This sharing strategy allows the church to reach more people, and the more people involved in sharing the church's information, the more exposure the church will get. The goal of sharing is to get the local community to see what God is doing at SOAR Church and can do in their lives. The SOAR Church has become known all over the county because of its social media strategy.

Community Involvement

The community must be a priority for any church that desires to grow. If a church wants to connect with the community, the church must be where the people are - in the community. Luke 14:23 "And the Lord said, unto the servant, 'Go out into the highways and hedges and compel them to come in that my house may be filled'." Too many churches are stuck in their buildings and leaders cannot grow a church with that approach. The church that has a community focus can use it to share the Gospel of Jesus. Engaging the community and using its resources can further your ministry to and within the community. The SOAR Church has successfully partnered with the law enforcement, community groups, local government, school districts, and other churches, and these partnerships equip the church to impact many areas in the county.

The church must be strategic about building relationships with key members of its community, however. These relationships can help the church with opportunities to do more ministry within its community. When the community sees a church as a resource, community members will come to you with opportunities to help people. The SOAR Church has been asked to assist in school issues, to help host seminars on community issues, to talk to local law enforcement officers on community relationships, to sponsor school events, to assist in cleaning local school facilities that have budget issues, and to help out in community concerns. When a church has a strategy for community, that strategy can provide the church an opportunity for an authentic presence in its community and contribute to the church's growth.

How to Sustain a Healthy Church?

When a church is growing, growth comes with many challenges. It must be noted that momentum can go both ways. A church can be moving forward and growing one moment; then things can change, and that same church can start to move toward a decline. In the Southern New Jersey and Philadelphia areas, several churches that had been growing over the past twenty years started to slow down and appeared to be stuck. Churches must avoid erosion, particularly slow erosion that takes place over time and often goes unnoticed by leaders until the situation becomes critical. Many churches that are in decline or are stagnant today were growing at one point during their history. The Gospel is alive today and the message to salvation is always the same, but the way church communicates these messages warrants change because society and cultures change, as do those in society the church is trying to reach. So, a church that was healthy at one time can suffer decline because of its refusal to change the way they communicate the Gospel message. If a church is going to stay relevant and healthy, it must reassess on a continual basis how it connects with people through its communication.

How does a church stay relevant and healthy during these times? Once a church is healthy, it must continue to do the necessary things to stay that way. First, the church must make sure that the Bible is its foundation. Everything that is done through the church must be based on the Bible. The church must be Bible Centric, which means that it will not do anything apart from the Word of God. A ministry that is Bible centered will continue to carry out its service for God. Romans 12:1 "Present your bodies a living sacrifice, holy, acceptable unto God, which is your reasonable service." When the church gets away from the Bible and from doing it God's way, it will start to decline. To have a healthy Bible-centered ministry starts with the members spending time with God. A church will be healthy when its membership is growing in the Word of God. II Timothy 2:15 "Study to shew thyself approved unto God, a workman that needeth not to be ashamed, rightly dividing, the word of truth." Paul, who was a tentmaker, knew the importance of cutting a straight line. If a line were not cut straight, it would produce a tent that would be difficult to stand. If the church is going to stand up right, then it must know the Word of God and how to communicate it during this time.

Second, the successful church must be devoted to Prayer. The early church in the Book of Acts prayed. Because they were committed to prayer, God did some great things through that church. Acts 2:42 "They devoted themselves to the apostles' teaching and to fellowship, to the breaking of bread and prayer." Again, if the church is going to stay healthy and grow, it must be committed to prayer. It is amazing to note that some churches do not put a priority on prayer. Prayer will produce power. If there is no prayer, then there is no power. Continual prayer not only during difficult times but good times as well should be a prime pillar of any church. There should be continued prayer for the pastor, leadership, vision, ministry planning, outreach, and the growth of the church.

Third, Use Technology. The church must understand and use technology if it is going to stay healthy. If a church uses technology effectively, then it will contribute to its growth. A healthy church is a growing church, a church that integrates technology so that it can reach people wherever they are and whatever types of learners they are. People use technology such as phones, tablets, and computers on a daily basis. Lena Kelly, who talks about Church Engagement for the 21st Century says, "The average person touches his phone an amazing 110 times a day.[45]" The church is living in a time of technology, and if the church is going to sustain its growth, it must understand and use technology on a continual basis. Having an online presence that pushes the Gospel messages, its services, its ministry. and outreach to the community is crucial to the health and growth of the church.

Quentin Schultze presented some statistics on why churches have decided to use media in worship. He says that media has and provides "84% more relevance to our members, 77% more relevance to youth, 66% for evangelism, 33 % keeping pace with other churches.[46]" He

---

[45] Lean Kelly. Church Engagement, How to keep your church relevant in the 21st century.

[46] Quentin Schultze. High-Tech Worship? "Using Presentational Technologies Wisely." Grand Rapids, MI.

believes that the church must engage tradition and the changes in culture where the Gospel message can be communicated vibrantly. Schultze maintains, "North American society has gone through somewhat a shift from print culture to an electronic culture.[47]" If society is shifting to electronics, then the church must shift also so that it can continues its growth and stays vibrant during this time.

Fourth, Plan Seasonally. The church needs to understand that every Sunday and every month do not look the same. Understand peak months and high traffic months. The SOAR Church is located in Southern New Jersey just five minutes from the beach. The summer months can be challenging because of the lure of the beach and summer jobs because of tourism. A healthy church will know it's challenging season so that it can plan accordingly. It is during the summer months that the SOAR Church will hold several community events designed to stay relevant during those three months. These events include fun day for the community, family and friend's day at church, a back-to-school event in the park, church picnic in the county park, and a partnering with other community organizations doing community outreach. The summer months can also be a challenge financially. So, the church needs to plan its budget to deal with those slow times.

The church should know its high attendance months. For the SOAR Church, those months are September through

---

[47] Quentin Schultze. High-Tech Worship? "Using Presentational Technologies Wisely." Grand Rapids, MI.

May. An effective plan and strategy capitalize during those times. because during those times things can be accomplished with attendance and ministry activity high. It is during the high attendance months that the leadership can cast vision, implement stewardship campaigns, increase ministry involvement, train leaders, impact local schools, and reach the community.

Fifth, Challenge people to serve. God has gifted people to serve in the Body of Christ. The Apostle Paul encouraged Timothy to use the gift that God had put in him. II Timothy 1:6 "I remind you to fan into flame the gift of God, which I send you through the laying on of my hands." The church must encourage people to serve because the church will struggle to grow if there are not workers. There must be a process that creates a healthy volunteer culture in the church. When people serve, they will stay engaged, and the church needs engaged people who carry out the mission of the church. Healthy volunteers will help the church to stay healthy.

Challenged people will help the church to reach the community. Staying connected to the community will help with church health and its continued growth. Engaging the community will help the church to grow in the future. A church will see its attendance grow when a community is involved. The early church grew when it drew in the community with the Gospel of Jesus Christ. If a church is going to sustain its growth, then it must know what process is needed. Every church does not operate the same way, but it must have some components that it needs to follow in order to sustain its growth. The church needs to remember that momentum changes quickly and can go in both ways.

Chapter 4
Results of Findings

Findings from Study

As a result of this book, I have concluded that the status of the many churches facing decline in membership has impacted the churches spiritually and physically. Not only has this problem grown over the years but it also appears to have gotten worse. It is a problem affecting denominations, associations, local churches, and communities. If this problem of decline continues to be ignored by most churches, then the Kingdom of God will suffer in the future because the Great Commission will not be carried out.

Revealed in the findings from this book are some unsettling issues that contributed to the decline and stagnation of many churches. The most surprising issue revealed was that of attendance – that is, people not attending church in the numbers they did in the past. There has been a significant drop off in membership in many churches because people across the country attend so sporadically, and that inconsistency in many cases has evolved into a non-attendance to houses of worship. This is a problem that is impacting all religions. Churches are suffering because of a lack of desire by many to attend houses of worship, thereby, resulting not only church decline but also church closure. Churches are closing because there are not enough people in the pew in most churches to sustain the physical building, to maintain the budget financially, and to do the work of the ministry.

The findings of this research for this book reflect the impact church decline and/or stagnation can have in the Southern New Jersey area specifically where some churches have closed, while others are on the verge of closing because of a membership decline. This condition leaves people floundering or adrift about their spiritual life whether they are aware of their spiritual dearth or not. Jeffery M. Jones of Gallup communicates that church membership has dropped the last two decades affecting religions across the board. He reports, "69% of U.S. adults were members of a church in 1998-2000, compared with 52% in 2016-2018.[48]" This is evidence that fewer people, nearly half the population in the United States, are going to church or any other house of worship; it appears that there is a trend toward no religion. Notice, the diagram below:

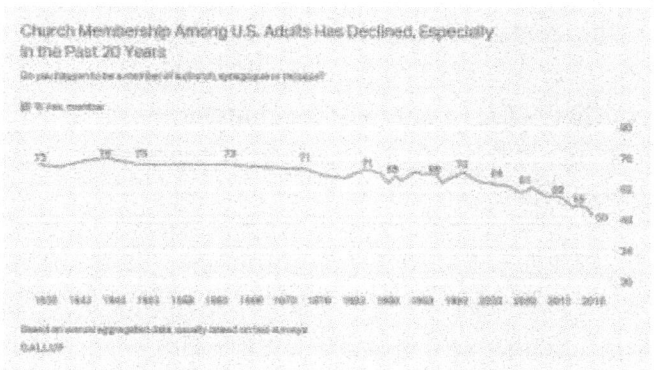

[48] Jeffery M. Jones. U.S. Church Membership Down Sharply. Gallup

As a result of my research, I have found the diagram to be true for the Southern New Jersey area as well. Churches that were once thriving churches in the area are now down to thirty members or fewer. They are barely surviving and could close their doors soon.

Another surprising issue revealed as a result of my research is that many leaders within declining churches are content with no growth; they are comfortable with their decline. Churches cannot move toward revitalization if leaders refuse to recognize the need for change in order to move the church forward. In addition, the constant conflict between pastors and leaders about the direction of the church has also hindered growth. One such instance this research detailed came from an interview with a Southern New Jersey area pastor who expressed his frustration over trying the move the church forward with a God-given vision. Encountering opposition from several leaders, this pastor found it hard to turn around this declining church and to begin a revitalization process. Such conflict is prevalent in other churches as well, especially in churches that were once thriving numerically and spiritually.

Thom S. Rainer warned that some churches are hindered in reversing their decline because the remaining members are blinded by the slow erosion that is taking place. Some leaders just do not see that their churches are in decline; hence, they refuse to address the situation. Rainer asserted, "Churches could have reversed the decline they were experiencing. But the remaining members in the church refused to see reality[49]." Often churches do not see the real possibility that they could close because of a lack of growth. It has been noted that several declining churches in Southern New Jersey are stuck or in decline because the remaining members refuse to change and are comfortable continuing to operate from the past. When pastors try to make a change from the past, they are met with opposition and resistance.

For example, another pastor in Southern New Jersey has been fighting his leaders for the past three years because they refuse to break with the church's past. This conflict has hindered growth and impaired the church's reputation in the community – the result: people have no desire to join the church. People do not want to be part of a church that is in constant turmoil. With most people worried about their needs getting met, with dealing with the pressures of life, and with needing answers to their problems, people would prefer to go to a church where their issues are being addressed than to be in a place where there is fighting over direction. Thom S. Rainer said, "The most pervasive and common thread of our autopsies was that the deceased churches lived for a long time with the past as hero. They often clung to things of the past with desperation and fear.[50]" The fear of change has hindered many churches from moving forward.

---

[49] Thom S. Rainer, Autopsy of the Church, B&H Publishing Group

[50] Thom S. Rainer, Autopsy of the Church, B&H Publishing Group

This research for this book found that several pastors in the Southern New Jersey area have grown frustrated because of conflict with leaders and the lack of growth taking place in the ministry. It is the desire of most pastors to grow the ministry where God has planted them. It can be difficult and disheartening when the calling is to help grow and expand the Kingdom of God, but they experience decline instead. In their frustration, a few have moved on to other churches or even resigned from ministry altogether.

Another issue that was noted is that it can be hard for the church going forward in the future if there is an absence of young people. The majority of declining churches in the Southern New Jersey area, specifically, and the United States of America, in general, experience the absence of young people ranging in age from 15 to 34. I have found that there was not only an absence of young people in declining churches, but also a difficulty in connecting with that 15-to-34-year-old group. That generation is being ignored or not accepted by some of these churches at all. The absence of an entire generation in most of these declining churches is detrimental but if these young people were present, that could help the churches to grow in the future. Many churches have lost their connection to that generation and, consequently, they have lost their futures.

This younger generation known as Millennials can be challenging to build a connection with, if churches do not understand how millennials operate in today's society. Tony Morgan talked about the difficulty in reaching millennials because they are less likely to claim any religious affiliation which has resulted in churches being "stuck" concerning this group. Pastors in the Southern New Jersey area have expressed a frustration about reaching this generation and many have given up on that group. Tony Morgan believes that this group is misunderstood but they can be reached and will contribute if approached the right way. He says, "Millennials get a bad rap. We hear leaders complain that they don't follow through, they get bored too easily and are too self-absorbed[51]." As a result, churches are coming up short when it comes to millennials, thus, their absence contributing to decline or stagnation.

Many thriving churches today have millennials who are active and involved in the ministry. Not all churches have lost the ability to reach millennials. These are churches that are connecting with this group and with entire families as a whole, which the church was designed to connect with. When a church understands the desires of millennials, then it can center some ministry activity around them. Once the millennials see their desires and needs met, they will get involved. They will see their own value to their church. Tony Morgan asserts, "Millennials are not just mindlessly living where they are, they care about their communities. They want to contribute and make a difference." Thriving churches will get millennials involved through community outreach, technology, creative arts, and small groups. If the church is going to

---

[51] Tony Morgan, The Unstuck Church, Thomas Nelson Publishers

reverse its decline or stagnation, then it must have a strategy to reach millennials.

My research has also found that not all churches in the country are stuck or in decline. There are many churches that are growing and thriving though they are all not mega. Instead, there are some small and medium-size ministries doing mega things. These churches are consistently growing and impacting their communities; they are in small rural towns where they are making an impact on those towns and areas. I have noticed that churches that are thriving have a plan and a strategy to stay relevant while so many churches that are declining have neither plan nor strategy. Thriving churches utilize technology, small groups, multiple campuses, community approaches, strong community involvement, ministries for all ages, shorter worship services, social media for outreach, and ministry marketing tools. Churches can thrive during this time if the right tools or methods are in place to connect with the people of this time.

Ideas from Study

Resultant ideas from this research could help turn around declining or stuck churches. For one, it is going to take churches working together and assisting each other if the church is going to turn this problem of decline or being stuck around. Second, this problem is not a denominational problem nor a local church problem - it is a Body of Christ problem. If one church is experiencing a problem of decline, then the entire Kingdom of God suffers because people are not being reached with the

Gospel of Jesus Christ. In addition, communities will suffer because needs will not be met and there will be no church in the community making an impact through its ministry. The church as a whole must come together and address this problem. Two ideas created from this study that can assist churches in correcting this problem are Partnerships and Mentorships.

Partnerships

There is a real need today for healthy churches that are thriving to come alongside declining or stuck churches. If partnerships are developed, then declining or stuck churches can benefit from partnering with healthy churches in ministry and help declining churches to become healthy again. There are some partnerships in existence doing ministry but not many partnerships walking with declining churches.

The Bible says in Proverbs 27:17, "Iron sharpens iron, so one person sharpens another." There is no church in the United States of America that is perfect. All churches could benefit from some type of partnership because all churches have areas of ministry that could be improved and strengthened. Every year thousands of Christian leaders attend conferences around the country designed to help them grow their ministries. The approach of partnerships provides an audience for struggling churches and the serious impact of this problem on so many churches.

The SOAR Church recently developed an area partnership with a church that was stuck. This struggling rural church has experienced little growth despite having a pastor that is skilled and knowledgeable in ministry and in leadership. However, the church lacked the people to do ministry. In reaching out, this rural church sought to create a partnership where the pastor would assist the SOAR Church in leadership development and ministry oversight. The SOAR Church would then assist this church in doing ministry in its community. Both churches would benefit from the partnership with the hope of growing in areas where each church needed help. So, partnerships are of value in that they will help healthy churches to become stronger and declining or stuck churches to experience growth.

Nate Smoyer in an article entitled "Seven Essentials to Creating Ministry Partnerships that Last" said, "Partnerships can be a powerful way for you to leverage your limited resources in ministry for the purpose of serving others.[52]" He believes that communities would benefit from partnerships. Healthy churches can help declining or stuck churches to make an impact in the communities where they serve. The results of this impact can help declining or stuck churches to become vibrant in their communities again, and community connection can help churches to experience growth. The SOAR Church has also developed partnerships with the local schools, law enforcement agencies, local community college, and community groups. These partnerships have allowed the

---

[52] Nate Smoyer. Seven Essentials to Creating Ministry Partnerships that Last. Orange Leaders.

church to make a bigger impact in the community and present those who are lost with the Gospel message.

Mentorships

The goal of mentorship would be that of healthy churches serving as mentors or trainers to declining or stuck churches. Healthy churches can serve as models imparting wisdom and skills that have been garnered over the years to grow their churches; healthy churches should not sit back while so many churches are struggling to survive. Mentorship can help many churches in the Body of Christ recover from this problem of decline.

Recently, the SOAR Church served as a mentor to a church in the Philadelphia area. This was a church that was struggling in growth and community ministry. After the SOAR Church shared its ideas, philosophy, and training with this church, it started to experience growth in the area of its membership and community outreach. The church, following the SOAR Church model regarding community outreach, has grown because of its ministry within the community. Mentorships can help declining churches to grow, thus, helping the entire Body of Christ in carrying out the Great Commission of reaching people for the Kingdom of God. If churches would help each other through partnerships and mentorships, then the problem of decline or stagnation would decrease over the next few years.

Beliefs from Study

It is this belief that the problem of church decline, or stagnation will get worse if it is not addressed soon. This book has presented statistics demonstrating that this problem has exacerbated over the past few years, and if not addressed, it will impact the church in a negative way because the Gospel message will not be evangelized to those who are lost. Luke 19:10: "For the Son of Man is come to seek and to save that which is lost." If the lost are not being reached with the Gospel, how can the church experience growth in the future? This is a problem that should be on high alert for the church community because of its harmful impact on the Gospel and the church community as a whole.

Second, there is a belief that this problem will demand more attention from religious organizations, associations, denominations, and churches because of the church closure rate that continues to climb. Churches are forced to merge in some religious circles because financially they cannot maintain their buildings due to decreased memberships, tithes, and offerings. Organizations, associations, and denominations are starting to give attention to the churches' needs because of their impact on these organizations, namely, the decrease in attendance and financial obligations to these organizations. The worse this problem gets, the more attention it will receive in the future.

Third, there is also a belief that this problem can be fixed in the future. There are organizations and church associations that are putting plans in place to address this problem. These plans, some presented in this research, can be effective if declining or stuck churches are committed to revitalization of their churches. It is a problem that definitely has solutions because churches around the country have been able to reverse their decline. When pastors and leaders work together, decline and stagnation can be fixed. Repair is going to take commitment, training, and an understanding of the problem in order to correct it. This research found that many declining churches simply do not have a plan or vision to reverse this problem, but churches that have a plan and vision are thriving. A church can survive with the correct leadership and plan in place.

Solutions from this Study

This book presented several solutions to the problem of decline in this study. The key to reversing this problem starts with the realization that there is a problem of decline in the church. I have noted that there are several organizations, denominations, and associations that have put plans and processes in place to assist churches in correcting this problem. It is up to the individual church to acknowledge that it has a problem and take the necessary steps to correct it. Unfortunately, there are churches that do not see their decline as a problem. The first step to correcting any problem is admitting that there is a problem. This is a problem that does not have to end in the closure of any church, however.

The book has presented health assessments, building blocks, strategies, and real-life scenarios that can be used to help turn around declining and stagnant churches. If a church applies some of these tactics and processes, it can be on the road to fixing its problem. However, this is not a problem that will be fixed overnight. It was noted in this research that correcting this condition is going to take commitment, hard work, teamwork, and time.

When one looks at solutions to this problem, he realizes it starts with change. First, churches must change their methods concerning ministry and outreach to their communities if this problem is going to be fixed. Too many churches that refuse to change with the times have become victims of decline. There is no avoiding change; it is something that everyone deals with in life. If churches are not careful, decline will be the consequence of their refusal to change. Ed Stetzer and Thom S, Rainer believe that change is necessary for churches to transform. They said, "We choose the kind of change that advances the Kingdom of God into our world, or we can retreat into a subculture that attempts to insulate us from the world.[53]" Churches that are thriving today have changed their methods, and those changes have helped them to advance the Kingdom of God in their communities. The churches that have refused to change have insulated themselves from their communities and are experiencing decline because of a lack of membership.

---

[53] Ed Stetzer and Thom S. Rainer. Transformational Church. B&H Publisher

Second, another solution is that of vision. This research has concluded that having a God- given vision is the key for any ministry to be successful. Every church that is going to thrive and grow during this season is going to need a vision and the right vehicle. Vision represents where the church is going, and the vehicle will help it to get there. A person can have a vision to get to London, but he lives in New York City and drives a BMW. The BMW is a great car, but it cannot get a person to London from New York City; it can only get an individual to the airport and will not fly nor travel over water. The traveler needs a vehicle that is suitable to get him to his destination. Often declining churches do not have the right vehicle that will help them to reach their destination. They need to find the right vehicle to manifest their vision to reach this generation and to grow the church. Too many declining churches are trying to do year 2019 ministry with 1980 vehicles resulting in decline or stagnation. Vision and vehicle are necessary for success.

Third, it was found in the research for this book that many declining churches have leadership problems. There are many stories about conflicts between the pastor and leadership, and these conflicts are evident in declining churches throughout the Southern New Jersey and Philadelphia areas. A church cannot grow where there is constant conflict, and this problem cannot be fixed by the pastor alone. He needs a leadership working with him to resolve this problem. Tony Morgan in *The Unstuck Church* asserts, "A pastor can't chart a course, plan effectively, and motivate his troops if his people aren't on board with his vision and core values[54]." Leadership must come together, or the decline will continue to exist and possibly close the church.

Fourth, churches must improve their community outreach. The church has been commissioned by God to spread the Gospel of Jesus Christ and to meet needs. I have found that most declining churches have no connection with their communities and no plan for evangelism. Churches are made up of the communities where they serve, and if the church has no relationship with its community, it will be hard for it to grow. I have seen declining churches in the Southern New Jersey area, churches where the community does not know they exist even though said churches may be big buildings on corners. The church must come up with creative ways to spread the Gospel to its community and to those who are lost. Having a connection with the community will grow any church.

Things to Be Achieved

Churches, organizations, denominations, and associations must be serious about correcting this problem. There must plans and processes outlined and developed to address this problem by the organizations that serve these churches. Along those lines of organization help, some declining churches in the Southern New Jersey area feel neglected by the religious organizations where they have memberships. These churches which have given faithfully

---

[54] Tony Morgan, The Unstuck Church. Thomas Nelson Publishers, Nashville, TN

to these organizations over the years are now in trouble and the organizations they partnered with either cannot help them or have not offered any help. Consequently, these churches are suffering a more serious decline and, because of a lack of help, are leaving the very organizations which promised assistance. Again, if this problem is going to be corrected, organizations, denominations, and associations must be committed to helping distressed churches remediate this problem as this problem not only impacts the local church but the religious organizations as well.

If local churches cannot find help from the religious affiliates and organizations that they have served for so many years, then they need to seek outside assistance from organizations that will help them to correct their problem of decline. Please note that this research has found there are organizations that not only will help but also want to help declining churches. The church community needs to communicate better to declining churches that it is ready to assist in correcting this problem; churches should not have to deal with his issue alone. I believe there are two things that need to be achieved concerning this problem in the future. First, there needs to be a plan in place to help declining churches, and second, there need to be some practices that declining churches will follow in the future.

Future Plans for Declining Church

In his book *Who Can Save the Incredible Shrinking Church?* Dr. Frank Page reported some sobering statistics regarding declining churches. He stated, "There are

400,000 congregations in America, over 340,000 are either plateaued or actually declining.[55]" It is clear based on these statistics that declining churches clearly outnumber thriving churches in the United States of America. This is a major problem that needs to be addressed, and plans need to be developed and implemented to combat this problem both now and in the future.

I have found that there is a scarcity of written materials to address the problem of church decline. More books and articles written to help churches resolve the problem is critical. Churches, pastors, associations, and denominations that have been successful with this problem need to communicate their strategies and practices to the church community. The church is a body, not an isolated entity unto itself; so, the entire church community needs to have some concern about correcting this problem. One strategy would be a yearly campaign by the church community to assist and engage the declining churches. There should be fear today that the number of declining churches will increase as the years move forward if there is no conversation begun about revitalization for these churches.

I have discovered that churches in decline in the Southern New Jersey area have never heard of church revitalization. Perhaps because numerous associations, denominations,

---

[55] Dr. Frank Page. Who Can Save the Incredible Shrinking Church?. Nashville TN: B&H Publishing Group

and organizations have failed to recognize the decline problem, and, thereby, have failed to communicate a plan for or resolution to declining churches; too many churches are left in the dark concerning this problem and do not know how to address it. Many of these churches have seniors who are love their church but cannot figure out how to initiate revitalization. Efforts to educate on this subject of revitalization of declining churches by the church community as a whole should be launched.

It is possible that declining churches can grow both spiritually and numerically. It will be a challenge, but success can be achieved if the right plan is created, developed, communicated, and executed. I believe that the following plan could help declining churches experience revitalization in the future.

First, denominations, associations, and healthy churches must come together, engage, and work hard to address this problem. Because this issue of decline impacts the church next door as well as the one across town, the Gospel is being hindered and evangelism is not going forward in cities or towns. Once a plan is designed that comes from healthy churches, associations, and denominations, these organizations should take the lead when it comes to helping churches adapt the plan and move toward correcting the church decline issue. Since many churches look up to these organizations for direction, this big problem that should be at the top of the organizations' agendas. These organizations can reach thousands of churches because of the partnerships that have formed, and no church that contributes financially and has a partnership with an organization should be left to suffer decline without some intervention. Romans 15:1: "We then that are strong ought to bear the infirmities of the weak, and not to please ourselves." It is important that the church community works together.

Second, denominations, associations, and healthy churches should start the revitalization dialogue with declining churches. Eventually, there should be no church in decline that is not aware of revitalization and what it consists of. It is imperative to create a national campaign to push the subject of revitalization especially when there are more churches in decline than churches that are growing. Such a state communicates that the church community has ignored some of its wounded. The BRN of the Southern Baptist Convention has started a dialogue on church decline this year educating churches in the Philadelphia and Southern New Jersey areas. The first phase of BRN's process is designed to reach all the churches in their areas - a long, far-reaching process reaching out to hundreds of churches can be started immediately.

Third, denominations, associations, and healthy churches should educate pastors on church decline and revitalization. Too many pastors are stuck when it comes to correcting this problem. My findings have indicated that many pastors, though they might realize the fact of church decline, do not know what to do to overcome this issue. Several pastors in the Philadelphia and Southern New Jersey area have expressed their desire to turn their churches around, but they are struggling with implementing a plan and process that will start growth within their ministries. A plan in place will assuredly help pastors to understand church decline and revitalization. If churches are going to turn around this problem, it will start with the pastors and their leaderships in understanding the severity of this problem and how to address it.

Fourth, denominations, associations, and healthy churches must be willing to walk churches through the process of reversing their decline issues. The recovery process should not stop at educating churches in the process but continue with a hands-on approach to assure churches that they will get the necessary help they need. The BRN of the Southern Baptist Convention has a team that will work with declining churches by walking churches through the process starting with health assessments. This association is necessary to assure declining churches that they have a partner to walk with them through the process.

Practices Used to Help Churches Recover

I believe that there are certain things that churches can do or change that will help them to recover from the problem of decline or stagnation. Churches need to do things that will help them to stay alive. Thom S. Rainer asserts, "Most churches move toward death because they refuse to acknowledge their condition.[56]" If churches are going to recover and move from decline, they need acknowledge they have a problem and do the necessary things to stay alive. Some necessary practices that declining churches

---

[56] Thom S. Rainer, Autopsy of the Church, B&H Publishing Group

can adopt that will help them to recover include a Welcoming environment, Disciple making, Sunday Morning, Ministry, and Marketing.

Focus on a Welcoming Environment

Joy Allmond wrote, "Most churches would double in size if they simply became friendly.[57]" Allmond visited many churches and her number one observation was that many churches were not friendly. When churches have a welcoming environment, it makes people feel good, welcome, and valued. The SOAR Church implemented a First Touch Ministry designed to greet everyone, including visitors, that walks through the front door with a hug and smile. It is called First Touch because members of that ministry are the first people to touch visitors. The first touch will make a difference in someone returning to your church. This ministry has received more compliments than any other ministry in the church. Churches that want to stay alive need to create a welcoming atmosphere that will make people feel loved and excited to be in their church.

Juan Sanchez wrote, "Guests notice and usually comment on how loving a fellowship is or is not by their willingness to welcome newcomers.[58]"

---

[57] Joy Allmond. 3 NON-Negotiables for Revitalizing a Dying Church. February 2019.

[58] Juan Sanchez. 10 Ways to Provide a Welcoming Environment for Your Guests This Easter. April 2017.

Some of the ways a church can welcome visitors are as follows:

- Greet everyone with a smile.

- Create Welcome signs for the parking lot.

- Create an inviting atmosphere; your church needs to be clean and decorated.

- Prepare a hospitality room for first time visitors. Prepare a gift for them.

- Invite first-time visitors to worship with you again.

- Present visitors with a package explaining what your ministry has to offer.

- Assist those visitors who do not seem to know where they are going.

- Introduce yourself to those you do not know.

Focus on Making Disciples

If a declining church is going to recover, then it must focus on disciple making, a top priority for every church. Too many churches have gotten away from making disciples, but churches grow by making disciples. There must be a strategy in place to reach and teach people about the Gospel of Jesus Christ. I have found that some declining churches in the Southern New Jersey area are more focused on annual programs than making disciples. Matthew 28:19-20: "Therefore, go and make disciples of all nations, baptizing them in the Name of the Father and of the Son and of the Holy Spirit," This is practice, if carried out, will help churches to recover and grow.

Focus on Sunday Morning

When churches have an impactful worship, it can make a difference. A church's Sunday morning worship is important for its growth. If the music, sermon, Sunday School classes, and atmosphere are not done with a Spirit of Excellence, there is a good chance that visitors will not return, and people will move on and try the next church. Sunday mornings need to be given much attention.

Dr. R. A. Vernon says, "My team and I spend hours preparing for over-weekend services[59]." If Sunday morning worship is going to be impactful, then everything must be planned out - the music, media, sermon, sound, and ministry must be planned out. The SOAR Church has weekly production meetings where the Sunday services are planned and discussed in detail. If declining churches are going to recover, one facet that must be focused on is Sunday morning services.

Focus on Ministry

If a church is going to recover from decline, ministry must be one of its prime focuses. When one looks at ministry, it

---

[59] Dr. R.A. Vernon Size Does matter: Moving Your Ministry from Micro to Mega. Victory Media & Publishing Company.

involves service on part of the believers. Ministry is people getting involved and serving others through the gifts that God has given them. A growing church will work to get everyone involved in ministry; however, if a church lacks ministry, then people's needs will not be met, and they will not grow spiritually. Ephesians 4:11: "For the perfecting of saints, for the work of the ministry, for the edifying of the body of Christ." Believers are fed to grow and mature in Jesus Christ for the purpose of the ministry, not to be surfeited and satisfied.

A growing church will have ministries based on Acts 2:41-47. It will have ministries for worship, fellowship, discipleship, and outreach. Churches that meet the everyday needs of the people will result in growth. Dr. R. A. Vernon relates, "Ask not what the world needs. Ask what makes you come alive; then go do it." He believes outreach caused his church to come alive. Every church needs to ask what ministry will make it come alive and then go do it.

Focus on Marketing

If declining churches are going to recover, then they need an identity in the community. Marketing one's church's ministry will help to answer the following question. "Why should I come to your church?" The community needs to know that your church exists. Most churches can grow if they are willing to work at a strategy that will help them to grow this type of marketing. Market your ministry in the following ways:

- Put the church's name or logo on shirts, hats, and jackets.

- Put the church name on cups and pens.

- Use invite cards to invite people to church.

- Have license plates imprinted with the church's name on it.

- Use social media to market ministry.

- Advertise in the local newspaper.

- Make use of radio.

- Utilize television.

Training that Needs to Be Done in the Future

The majority of pastors today serve in a church that is in decline or in stagnation. Even so, most pastors are trying to carry out their God-given calling but are ministering in churches that are struggling to stay alive. One of the greatest hopes today is to see churches make a comeback from their decline or stagnation, along with the hope that pastors will minister in healthy, thriving churches. Most pastors did not go into their God-given calling expecting some of the challenges of growing a church. It can be discouraging, depressing, and frustrating mentally dealing with something that is dying that you want it to grow.

Training will help pastors and their leadership who desire to see their churches make a comeback.

There should be training for pastors and their leadership by the organizations that serve them whether through conferences, seminars, or webinars on revitalization. Pastor and leaders need to be trained and educated on revitalization as there is not enough information educating pastors on revitalization. Revitalization, which means to give something new life, a fresh start, communicates a process of making something grow or become successful again. Pastors need to be educated in processes and plans that will help their churches to grow again, to become successful again. The word "Revitalization" should be the key word spoken in churches all over the United States of America. Pastors and churches need to get an understanding of this topic so that churches can understand that there is hope in getting their church a fresh start.

Andrew M. Davis in his book entitled *Revitalize, Biblical Keys to Helping your Church Come Alive Again* says, "A church that has been dying for a long time will be rescued only by revitalization. As dangerous and painful as church revitalization can be, the far greater danger is not revitalizing.[60]" It is very important that a dialogue start on the topic of revitalization with pastors and their churches.

---

[60] Andrew M. Davis. Revitalize "Biblical Keys to Helping Your Church Come Alive Again". Baker Books

Training on the importance of church growth is often overlooked. The research for this book has found too many churches are content with no growth taking place, but if things are alive, they should grow. So, it stands to reason that the church should be alive and growing because it is a living organism. Church growth started with the Great Commission found in Matthew 28:18-20; the commission signifies growth not stagnation. Furthermore, Carey Neiuwohf wrote, "Many churches settle for mediocrity.[61]" Churches cannot allow the past, traditions, or a lack of understanding to stand in the way of growth, progress, and greatness. Churches must be trained on how to grow because change occurs daily, and they must be ready to meet the challenges of change.

There also needs to be training on how to reach the Millennial generation. With the disconnect with many churches suffer on how to reach millennials, churches must be educated in the methods to attract, reach, and keep this generation or more churches will decline in the future. Tony Morgan reasons, "If you were going to be a missionary to a village in the Amazon for the next twenty years, you would start by learning the language, understanding their customs and tools, and figuring out how the people live and make sense of their world.[62]" It is the same with millennials; if the church is going to reach

---

[61] Neiuwhof, Carey, Lasting Impact "7 Powerful Conversations that will help your church grow", The Rethink Group, Cumming, GA.

[62] Tony Morgan. Reaching and Leading Millennials. Thomas Nelson. Nashville, TN.

them, it has to get an understanding of how they operate in today's society. The church must be trained on how to reach and communicate with this generation because they can be used by God to reach others of their generation.

Chapter 5
Conclusions

Summary of Findings

This book has presented several questions that need to be answered. The hope is that this book was able to answer those questions and provide strategies to help churches recover from decline or stagnation. The questions are as follow:

Does Church Decline really exist in America? This book has demonstrated that church decline is a problem with the majority of churches in America and that this decline has impacted many churches and communities across America. It is a problem that has been in existence and percolating for years but has gone relatively undetected until recently. An alarming statistic which revealed just how big this problem is in America is that of the 400,000 churches in America, 340,000 of them either in stagnation or decline. The far-reaching, alarming impact is that 85% of pastors are serving in churches that have some type of struggle to grow.

This is a problem that has been debilitating on the occupation of pastoring, causing pastors to struggle over their calling to serve in this area. Though this is just one of many problems that pastors face on a daily basis, it may be the toughest. Everyone wants to be successful in whatever task that is before him. However, the stark reality is that decline and/or stagnation can happen at any level or during any number of years in the pastorship.

Recently, a senior pastor shared how he has served as senior pastor in the Southern New Jersey area for 30 years. He said his church has been in decline recently, a situation which has broken his heart because he has not been able to turn it around. It has caused much stress on his life, with the fear of his ministry coming to an end. This is a problem that not only impacts churches and communities but leaders who desire to serve as well.

This book noted that the biggest cause of church decline is a loss of membership. When people leave the church, it puts it in a very bad situation. Consequently, when membership declines, it leads to the church's decline. In other words, churches are not able to maintain their buildings, their ministries, and their finances because of a lack of funds and a lack of people. It was reported in this research that, as a result of this condition, many churches are closing or merging because they do not have the membership to maintain their buildings or ministries. This is a problem that is being experienced across many Houses of Worship in America.

Another reason noted for decline is that people do not attend Houses of Worship consistently or at all anymore. It appears that people have lost interest in religion, and because of people's lack of interest, the church today is struggling with reaching people and growing ministries. If the church is going to deal with this problem of decline, then it has to come up with creative ways to reach people. The research has found that there are some churches that are effective and are not experiencing decline. These churches have found solutions that have helped them to be impactful and healthy while many churches have struggled.

Is there help for Declining Churches in America? This problem of decline or stagnation is finally beginning to get the attention that it needs because of its impact on churches, communities, associations, and denominations. Some of these organizations are starting to take the necessary steps to correct this problem. For example, some denominations, associations, and organizations are holding and engaging in seminars, training, conversations, and consultations with pastors and leaders in declining churches. These organizations are giving health assessments and strategies that will help declining churches to recover. If a church wants help, help being offered to those who desire it.

There are consultants who are willing to come alongside churches and walk them through the recovery process. Because of the impact of this problem, there is a need for more consultants who have a desire to help churches to correct this problem. I believed that more consultants would come forward as the awareness of this problem grows.

In addition, there are books and articles written that are designed to help churches to recover. The more attention this problem gets, the more books and articles will be written addressing the issue plaguing the declining churches. Many of these books and articles outline the necessary steps to recover from this problem and to experience revitalization.

Even with the tools, resources, and aides in existence today, there needs to be more help for those churches in states of decline and stagnation. It remains a problem that is still being ignored by too many organizations. The church community needs to become more educated, more involved, and more committed to this problem so that the help can reach all churches who desire to recover from this problem.

Can Declining Churches experience growth again? There is a belief from this research that churches can recover from this problem and experience growth again. God will supply the church with what it needs to recover if a church so desires. Philippians 4:13 "I can do all things through Christ that strengthens me." I not only believe but have seen God provide the church with what it needs to recover. The SOAR Church was a picture of a declining church but recovered with God sending it the resources that it needed to recover. Declining churches are going to need to use available resources such as training, books, articles, and assistance from healthy churches and outside organizations. It is going to take a united effort from several areas to help declining churches to recover.

This book has presented material that has shown the church can recover from this problem, and that this is not a problem that cannot be corrected. It just needs attention, direction, support, and focus from organizations and healthy churches who are in a position to help. It needs the pastor and leadership working together to move the church toward revitalization.

Andrew M. Davis in his book *Revitalize* stresses that God can speak life into a dying church. He says, "Revitalization occurs when God restores a once healthy church, helping it to change course from its recent decline toward spiritual disease and death.[63]" Declining churches must allow God to speak to them so that restoration can take place. Andrew M. Davis gives the example of Ezekiel 37 where God speaks to dry bones, doing the same for declining churches helping them to revitalize.

Ed Stetzer in his book *Comeback Churches* says, "you cannot save a church without focusing on the important things that make a church.[64]" The church must make sure that it has not gotten away from the purpose of the church, which is to spread the Gospel of Jesus Christ, and to make disciples. Declining churches can make a comeback today through revitalization.

Are there strategies and processes that can help declining churches to recover? This book has presented some strategies and processes that can help declining churches to recover. These strategies include the importance of vision implementation, leadership development, development of a ministry plan, community connection, and incorporation of social media. There are also books and articles containing material for churches to aid in their recovery from decline or stagnation. The partnership with

---

[63] Andrew M. Davis. Revitalize "Biblical Keys to Helping Your Church Come Alive Again". Baker Books.

[64] Ed Stetzer. Comeback Churches. B&H Publishing Group.

organizations, associations, and denominations is vital in seminars presentations of strategies designed to help churches in the process of revitalization.

Thom S. Rainer highlights some responses that can help dying churches to recover. He mentions that the church must confess its needs. He says, "Most churches move toward death because they refuse to acknowledge their condition.[65]" Secondly, he believes that the church must pray for wisdom and strength to make the necessary changes. Thirdly, the church must be willing to change radically. He says, "The church has to change decades of cumulative problem behaviors in a very short time.[66]" Recovery will take time and the church cannot waste time moving through the process. Finally, he believes that change must lead to action. Too many churches are talking about change but are not acting on change. There must be movement if the process is going to take place and be successful. God honors movement.

Andrew M. Davis talked about different strategies that will help declining churches to recover. He presents that the church must embrace God's ownership of the church before he can start the recovery process. Too many in the church have gotten away from an understanding that the members are just stewards, or managers, of God's house. He says, "A passion for the exaltation of Christ as head over the church must enflame the heart of all church

---

65 Thom S. Rainer, Autopsy of the Church, B&H Publishing Group

66 Thom S. Rainer, Autopsy of the Church, B&H Publishing Group

revitalizers.[67]" If there is no passion for the purpose of the church, then it will be hard to start a recovery process. Andrew M. Davis also mentioned some additional tenets such as holiness, reliance on God, prayer, humility, courage, patience, and leadership development. These practices along with the strategies mentioned in this research can help declining churches to recover. The church must believe in Matthew 19:26 "With men this is impossible but with God all things are possible."

Do Pastors have the necessary training on church Decline? I believe that there is not enough training for pastors and leaders on the subject of declining churches. All pastors and leaders need to be educated on this problem and its resolution even if they are not presently in that dilemma. Many churches are suffering with decline or stagnation because there is a lack of knowledge concerning this problem which has the potential to affect all churches. Too many associations, denominations, and organizations are not focused on educating its churches on how to deal with this problem, and research findings indicate there needs to be a bigger focus on helping churches to overcome. Many pastors are dealing with so many problems on a daily basis and have no solutions; it would help greatly and allay the magnitude of these problems if there were more public information to deal with this problem of decline.

---

[67] Andrew M. Davis. Revitalize "Biblical Keys to Helping Your Church Come Alive Again". Baker Books.

Also, healthy churches need to serve as resources to pastors and their leadership who are experiencing decline. The church community needs healthy churches to get involved in helping its brothers and sisters to recover. The church community cannot afford to be selfish when it comes to helping to fix this problem. It is going to take everyone working together to correct the problem of decline.

Going forward, there needs to be more training available for pastors, equipping them to deal with church decline. The training should focus on revitalization, vision implementation, leadership development, ministry planning, community outreach, and Sunday morning worship. If pastors are not equipped to deal with the problem of church decline, more churches will suffer and possibly close. If pastors are equipped, then churches will become better equipped to deal with this problem of decline and pay it forward by helping other churches. The office and responsibility of pastor is the key ingredient to the ministry. Jeremiah 3:15 "And I will give you pastors according to Mine heart, which shall feed you with knowledge and understanding."

Suggestions for Future Research

There are topics that can help churches to better understand decline and stagnation. Also, these topics can help churches to continue growth after their recovery process. There needs to be continued research in the future on church decline and other topics relating to this issue, so that these problems are avoided in the future. Some topic suggestions for future research are Church Revitalization, Reaching Millennials, Contemporary Worship, Community Connection, and Understanding Church Growth.

Church Revitalization

It is difficult for churches to recover from stagnation and decline if there is no understanding of revitalization. Again, revitalization means to restart, to refresh, or to give new life. Churches that are in decline need to understand how to give their church new life again. Andrew M. Davis describes revitalization as "an effort to restore Biblical means to a once healthy church from disease to a state of spiritual health[68]." Once churches are educated on how to bring their churches back to life again through a revitalization process, they can successfully make that recovery.

Thom S. Rainer believes that many churches are in need of revitalization. There are too many churches that are not moving forward and could close if revitalization is not started. Thom S. Rainer says, "Because many churches have been negligent about reaching beyond their own walls, they lack the knowledge to know how to get out of the rut and revitalize.[69]" Because numerous churches do not know the next steps to correct the problem of decline,

---

[68] Andrew N. Davis. Revitalize. Baker Publishing Group.

[69] Thom S. Rainer. Ten Roadblocks to Church Revitalization.

research on this topic will be important for all churches in the future.

I understand that every church is different and could be declining for different reasons. Future research on revitalization could present and address the many scenarios that churches may be encountering today. A future study will help churches by making information available to them along with the many strategies on how to revitalize their church. Research on this topic could help churches to recover quicker because they will have a process and strategies available to them.

Reaching Millennials

Many declining churches have a problem reaching the Millennial generation. This is a generation that is challenging and, at the same time, contributing to the decline of many churches because of their absence. This generation is the future church, but churches will have no future if they do not develop an understanding on how to engage this generation. A future study that will educate and train churches on how to reach and engage the Millennial generation is crucial. This is a generation that cannot be ignored because of their impact on the future of the church. Many declining churches in the Southern New Jersey area not only have no Millennial generation in attendance but also have no desire to reach them. These churches are filled with seniors and could close in the near future because they lack young people.

Tony Morgan says, "Millennials are not just mindlessly living where they are; they care about their communities.

They want to contribute and make a difference.[70]"
Millennials can make a difference in any church, one in
particular, the SOAR Church. The SOAR Church has seen
Millennials develop mentor ministries for other young
people and make a tremendous impact for the church.
They have been very creative in developing ministries and
attracting other Millennials to the church. Churches that
are declining today must understand that millennials can
contribute and help the ministry to grow. Future study can
show churches how to relate and use them in ministry;
churches need Millennials so that they can have a future.

Contemporary Worship

Needed also is a future study on worship that is known as
contemporary in some circles. Contemporary worship is
not traditional and is different from the worship of the
past. Contemporary worship styles are growing. What is
contemporary worship? It can be described as a worship
service that is fast paced, heavy on music; uses drama,
theater lights, production; and uses social media. The use
of visual projection equipment is utilized more in
contemporary worship than in a church with a traditional
ministry style. There are worship teams, non-traditional
instruments such as keyboards, guitars, and horns, and
casual dress for both the pastor and the membership.

It is believed that the traditional style of worship has
caused a decline in many churches because it is not

---

[70] Tony Morgan. Reaching and Leading Millennials. Tyndale House
   Foundation.

attracting the younger generation. Numerous growing churches attribute their growth to this contemporary style of worship. According to USA Today, writer by Cathy Lynn Grossman says, "U.S. churches are marching to their own drum more than ever.[71]" She believes that some churches have disconnected themselves from denominational ties and rules that have blocked change and growth. There are nearly 50 % of Protestant churches using electrics guitars, drums, lighting, and media presentations during worship services. These churches have grown from 35 % since the year 2000. Many believe that this is necessary as times have changed. This will be important research in the future because it will help churches to better understand its impact on society.

Community Connection

Most churches that need revitalization are not aware of the makeup and needs communities where they are located. Churches are stuck in the buildings having little desire to connect with the community. A lack of awareness about the community can contribute to any church's decline. If the church is not sharing the Gospel of Jesus Christ and carrying out the Great Commission, how can the church grow? Available research on the importance and effectiveness of churches having community connections could be the springboard to recovery and revitalization. A

---

[71] Cathy Lynn Grossman, U.S. Churches are marching to their own drum more than ever. USA Today.

failure to connect will contribute to a church decline or stagnation.

A future research on this topic can help churches to better connect with the communities they serve. A church that grows relationships in the community will be able to meet the needs of that community. Jeremiah 29:7 "Seek the peace and prosperity of the city to which I have carried you into exile. Pray to the Lord for it, because if it prospers, you too will prosper."

Tony Morgan says, "Sometimes we become fixated on being the best church in the community, rather than being the best church for our community.[72]" The church must have an impact on the community where it is planted and not be some invisible entity when it comes to the community outreach. The book *Scrappy Church* by Thom S. Rainer tells the story of a church that was in decline and how it changed its approach and began to focus on community outreach. The story reports that 80% of this community was not in church, but when this church devoted resources to the Great Commission, they saw their decline change to a vibrant church. He reported that this church said, "The more we devoted our time and money to reach others, the more we saw our impact on the community. The church is now a vibrant congregation serving its community.[73]" A community connection can

---

[72] Tony Morgan. Stuck in a Funk. Tyndale House Foundation. Carol Stream, IL.

[73] Thom S. Rainer. Scrappy Church. B&H Publishing. Nashville, TN.

help declining churches experience growth, and future research on this topic can help churches to understand the importance of having a community connection.

Tony Morgan reported that there was one key attribute of churches that are in decline. He says, "When churches become inward-focused and start making decisions about ministry to keep people rather than reach people, they also start to die.[74]" Churches cannot stay stuck in the building and expect growth. It is imperative that there be a focus on reaching the community with the Gospel of Jesus Christ. A church with a community connection can reach the lost for Jesus Christ. Most of our communities are filled with unsaved people. How can these people be reached if there is no connection to the community allowing the church to carry out the Great Commission?

Understanding Church Growth

Research on the topic of church growth will help declining churches to see and understand the importance of growing a church. Every church should have a desire to want to grow its church. Unfortunately, I have seen too many declining churches that are comfortable with not growing. Too many declining congregations have become satisfied with being in the state of decline; there is no attempt to grow their membership. It is God's desire for every church

---

[74] Tony Morgan. The Unstuck Church. Thomas Nelson Publishers. Nashville, TN.

to grow because He gave them the Great Commission in Matthew 28:18-20, which is to go and make disciples.

If churches would gain an understanding of church growth, then it is possible that there would be fewer churches in decline. The more churches that are growing, the fewer churches there would be in decline. This topic is important because it would educate church leadership on the importance of church growth and that the Bible requires it to grow and make disciples. The church started in Acts 2, with twelve disciples and has now grown to millions of believers today. If the church focuses on church growth, God will bring about an increase. Church growth must be considered a top priority for all churches.

Conclusion: What Has Been Learned?

This book has revealed some serious issues about declining churches that were not known to me prior. The problem of decline is bigger than most in the church community are aware of. So many churches have grown so comfortable with membership decline that they no longer see decline as a problem. Based on the statistics that were reported, this is a problem that continues to grow every year. It is a problem that will grow and get worse over time if there is no resolution or attempt by the church community to correct it. This research revealed that this problem has been around for decades but has gotten worse lately. It will intensify over time if this problem is not addressed soon by the church community.

The surprise was to learn that so many Denominations, Associations, and Organizations have ignored this problem, and some continue to even today. This problem of decline has not gotten the attention it deserves, and it is unbelievable that organizations can see churches in decline and do nothing to correct it. Although this research has revealed that there are some organizations moving to address this problem, not enough are considering the huge, far-reaching impact on the church community. Also, it is a problem with few resources available to address this problem, and resources are needed to help churches understand this problem and address it. Denominations, Associations, and Organizations need to make this problem a top priority, requiring immediate attention because of its impact on the church community. The Great Commission is being hindered by this problem.

The most alarming problem revealed by this research was that of 85% of pastors are serving in churches that are in decline, struggling to move forward, or in stagnation. This problem is hard on the life of the pastor and his family presenting challenges resulting in some pastors resigning, changing churches, and some committing suicide. Pastors have to deal with an abundance of problems on a daily basis ranging from their own personal life issues to the struggles of growing a ministry. This is a problem where pastors need help from outside the church; this would help take some of the pressure of this problem off their lives. Many in the congregation do not know the daily challenges in the life of a pastor, challenges like leaders and members who fight change, question vision, and criticize every decision. Churches must understand the importance of assisting the pastor with the work of the ministry.

I also learned that this big problem can be corrected if churches are committed to turning it around. There are leaders and organizations in the church community who want to see this problem fixed, and any church that wants help on this problem can find it. It is my hope that more churches and organizations come forward providing help to assist churches in recovery from this problem. The research for this book has been an eye opener, and my prayer is that the church community will step up quickly to aid churches in their recovery before more churches are impacted by it in the very near future.

How can this research improve the churches that have experienced this problem?

My prayer is that this project has helped some church or pastor concerning the problem of decline. I believe that this project can help churches that are experiencing this problem to recover in the near future. It is a problem that will take time but can be fixed with the right strategy and plan in place. It will also take a commitment from the entire church community.

I believe that this project can help to educate pastors and churches on a problem that is impacting so many in the church community. Because of the education regarding this problem, pastors and churches will not only see the need to correct this problem in the future but will also realize that if this problem is not corrected, it can have damaging consequences. The hope is that churches will improve their knowledge of this problem and will be aware of it moving forward. It is also the hope that churches will learn to work together to conquer this problem, a problem that seriously impacts that entire Body of Christ.

This research has presented strategies that can help churches recover. My prayer is that churches can use these strategies to assist them in correcting their problem of decline, a problem that can be fixed with the right plan in place. This book was designed to present material that any church can apply to their situation and experience recovery. My hope is that this research will help churches recognize decline, recover from decline, experience growth, and impact the communities where they are located. It is my desire to see churches recover and become healthy again. The world needs more healthy churches because there are too many people that are lost without the Gospel of Jesus Christ.

Finally, it is my hope that pastors are encouraged by this project. Prayerfully, pastors will be inspired to attack this problem and see the hand of God working in their lives and in ministry again. God is not done with the church just yet and we are excited about the churches that will recover in the future because of this project.

Bibliography

Allmond, Joy. 3 Non-Negotiables for Revitalizing a Dying Church. 2019

Baker, Jonny & Doug Gray. Alternative Worship "Resources from and for the Emerging Church." Grand Rapids, MI, Baker Books: 2004

Barna, George & Kinnaman David. Churchless. Tyndale House Publishers Inc.

Benson, Dennis C. The Visible Church. Nashville TN: Abingdon Press 1988

Bock, Susan, K. Liturgy for the Whole Church "Resources for Multigenerational Worship." New York, NY, Church Publishing Incorporated: 2008

Bradley, D. Jayson. 6 Important Church Attendance Statistics and What they tell. Bellingham, WA.

Chand, Samuel R. Cracking Your Church's Culture Code: Seven keys to unleashing Vision and Inspiration. San Francisco, CA: Jossey-Bass, 2011

Collins, John. Built to Last "Successful Habits of Visionary Companies." Collins Business Essentials. Boulder, CO: 1994

Davis, Andrew. Revitalize, Biblical Keys to Helping Your Church Come Alive Again. Baker Books, Grand Rapids, MI: 2017

Davis, Josh & Lerner, Nikki. Worship Together in church as in heaven. Nashville, TN, Abingdon: 2015

Dawson. Thomas. An Examination of Pastoral Leadership in African American Churches Today. Langhorne, PA Philadelphia College of Bible: 1997

Dodd, Brian. The 2-Minute Leader "10 Indispensable Practices." Spire Resources Inc. Camarillo, CA: 2013

Duck, Ruth, C. Worship for the Whole People of God "Vital Worship for the 21st Century." Louisville, KY: 2013

Erlandson, Doug. Spiritual Anorexia "How Contemporary Worship is Starving the Church." Grand Rapids, MI, Zondervan: 2011

Evans, Tony, Let's Get to Know Each Other. Nashville, TN. Thomas Nelson Publishers 1995.

Finzel, Hans. The Top Ten Mistakes Leaders Make. Wheaton, IL, Victors Books: 1990

Franklin, Jentezen. Take Hold of your Dream. Lake Mary, FL, Charisma House: 2011

Furtick, Steven. Greater "Dream bigger, Start smaller. Ignite God's Vision for Your Life. Multnomah Books. Colorado Springs CO: 2012

Greenslade, Philip. Leadership, Greatness and Sevanthood. Minneapolis, MN. Bethany House Publishers

Grier, T. William. The mission of the Church, Philadelphia, PA: Int'l City: 1989

Hybels, Bill. Courageous Leadership. Expanded edition. Grand Rapids, MI: Zondervan: 2009.

Henard, Bill. Reclaimed Church. Nashville, TN B&H Publishing Group 2018

Kimball, Dan. Emerging Worship "Creating Worship Gatherings for New Generations." Grand Rapids, MI: Zondervan Press: 2004

Kotter, John, P. A Sense of Urgency. Harvard Business Press. Boston MA: 2008

Leighton, F. Transforming Leadership. Downers Grove, IL, Inter Varsity Pres: 1991

Liesch, Barry. The New Worship "Straight Talk on Music and the Church." Grand Rapids, MI, Baker Books: 2001

London, B. H. Jr. & Wiseman B. Neil. The Heart of a Great Pastor "How to grow strong and thrive wherever God has planted you." Ventura, CA, Regal Books: 1994

MacArthur, John, Jr. Shepherdology. Sun Valley, CA: Grace: 1977

Mac Arthur John, Jr. Rediscovering Pastoral Ministry. Waco, TX, Word Publishing: 1995

Marti, Gerardo. Worship Across the Racial Divide. New York, NY. Oxford Press: 2012

Mattson, Ralph, T. Visions of Grandeur "Leadership that creates positive Change." Chicago, IL, Moody Press: 1994

Neiuwhof, Carey, Lasting Impact "7 Powerful Conversations that will help your church grow", The Rethink Group, Cumming, GA.

Maxwell John. 21 Irrefutable Laws of Leadership, Thomas Nelson Publisher, Grand Rapids, MI.

Means, James, E. Effective Pastors for a New Century. Grand Rapids, MI: Baker Books: 1993

Miller, Steve. The Contemporary Christian Music Debate. "Worldly Compromise or Agent of Renewal? Wisdom Creek Press. Acworth GA: 2011

Morgan, Tony. The Unstuck Church, Thomas Nelson Publishers, Nashville, TN.

Morgan, Tony. Reaching and Leading Millennials, Thomas Nelson Publishers, Nashville, TN.

Muck, Terry. When to take a Risk "A guide to Pastoral Decision Making." Waco, TX, Word Books: 1987

Ortlund, Anne. UP with Worship "Hot to Quit Playing Church." Nashville, TN, Broadman and Holman Publishers: 2001

Page, Frank Dr. Who Can Save the Incredible Shrinking Church?. Nashville TN: B&H Publishing Group: 2010

Pitts, M. Johnathan, Church Merge, Close. Baltimore Sun.

Rainer, S. Thom. Autopsy of a Deceased Church. Nashville TN: B&H Publishing Group: 2014

Rainer, S. Thom. Breakout Churches. Grand Rapids, MI. Zondervan: 2005

Rainer, S Thom. Scrappy Church. B&H Publishing. Nashville, TN: 2017

Sanchez, Juan. 10 Ways to provides a Welcoming Environment for Your Guests This Easter. 2017

Schaller, Lyle E. The Very Large Church. Nashville TN: Abingdon Press: 2000

Schultze, Quentin. High-Tech Worship? "Using Presentational Technologies Wisely." Grand Rapids, MI. Baker Books: 2004

Schmidt, Wayne. Ministry Momentum "How to get it, Keep it and Use it in your Church." Indianapolis, IN, Wesleyan Publishing House: 2004

Sealey, Benjamin. Restoring the Heart of Worship. Benjamin Sealey Press: 2014

Smoyer, Nate. Seven Essentials to Creating Ministry Partnerships that Last. Orange Leaders 2015.

Stetzer Ed & Thom S. Rainer. Nashville, TN: Transformational Church. B&H Publishing Group: 2010.

Stewart, F. Carlyle. African American church growth "Twelve principles for prophetic ministry." Nashville TN: Abingdon Press: 1994

Sweet, Leonard I. Piloting Your Church in Today's Fluid Culture. Colorado Springs CO: Group Publishing: 1999

Towns, L. Elmer. The of today's most Innovative Churches "What they're doing? How they're doing it? Ventura, CA: Regal Books: 1990

Tripp, David P. Dangerous Calling "Confronting the Unique Challenges of Pastoral Ministry." Wheaton, IL. Crossway: 2012

Vernon, R. A. Size Does Matter "Moving your ministry from micro to mega." Cleveland, OH: Victory Publishing Company: 2011

Wallace, Robin K. Worshipping in the Small Membership Church. Nashville, TN, Abingdon Press: 2008

Warren, Rick. The Purpose Drive Church. Grand Rapids Mi: Zondervan: 1995

Warren, Rick. Growth is Okay, But Church Health is What Matters. Church Leaders, 2018.

Young, Ed. The Creative Leader: Unleashing the Power of your Creative Potential. Nashville, TN: Broadman & Holman Publishers: 2006

Zuck, Roy, B. Vital Ministry Issues. Grand Rapids MI, Kregel Resources: 1994